DK EYEWITNESS

T0001830

TOP **10**
BARCELONA

Top 10 Barcelona Highlights

The Top 10 of Everything

CONTENTS

Barcelona Area by Area

Streetsmart

Within each Top 10 list in this book, no hierarchy of quality or popularity is implied. All 10 are, in the editor's opinion, of roughly equal merit.

Title page, front cover and spine The striking *mosaic-covered Gran Plaça Circular, Park Güell;* *back cover, clockwise from top left* Ceiling of *Palau de la Musica Catalana; Barceloneta Beach;* *outdoor restaurants, Plaça Reial; Park Güell;* *Museu Nacional d'Art de Catalunya*

Welcome to
Barcelona

On the shores of the Mediterranean, the Catalan capital sizzles with creativity. Dramatic Modernista structures stand amid grand medieval quarters in an aesthetic juxtaposition of old and new. Across town, cutting-edge design, a vibrant art scene and delectable cuisine serve up a feast for the senses. With DK Eyewitness Top 10 Barcelona, it's yours to explore.

For all its apparent big-city bustle, Barcelona is a place to linger, whether on the palm-shaded seafront, over coffee in a medieval square or picnicking at **Park Güell** or in a **Montjuïc** garden. The best way to experience the city is on foot, getting lost in the labyrinthine alleyways of **Barri Gòtic** or taking time to notice the details – ceramic garlands, wrought-iron balustrades, vibrant tiles – on the **Eixample** Modernista mansions. The streets are full of **public art**, from Haring murals to Lichtenstein sculptures, and there are a host of fantastic **museums** dedicated to Picasso, Miró, contemporary art and more.

Modern Catalan cuisine is both innovative and daring, and alongside molecular gastronomy in award-winning restaurants, you'll also find some places serving fabulous local produce the way they've done for generations. At the colourful local festivals, you'll get an insight into what makes Barcelona so different from the rest of Spain. Instead of flamenco dancing, you can admire the locals as they dance the *sardana* or watch the *capgrossos* (fatheads) process through the streets.

Whether you're coming for a weekend or a week, our Top 10 guide brings together the best of everything that the city has to offer, from Gaudí's finest masterpieces – the **Sagrada Família** and **Casa Batlló** – to the 18th-century maze in **Parc del Laberint d'Horta**. The guide has useful tips throughout, from seeking out what's free to places off the beaten track, plus nine easy-to-follow itineraries, designed to tie together a clutch of sights in a short space of time. Add inspiring photography and detailed maps, and you've got the essential pocket-sized travel companion. **Enjoy the book, and enjoy Barcelona**.

Clockwise from top: Museu Nacional d'Art de Catalunya, stained-glass dome at the Palau de la Música Catalana, La Pedrera's chimneys, entrance to Park Güell, Casa Batlló's windows, maze at the Parc del Laberint d'Horta, plaça outside Basílica de la Mercè, Barri Gòtic

Exploring Barcelona

You'll be utterly spoiled for choice for things to see and do in Barcelona, which is packed with historical buildings, parks, museums and beaches. Whether you're coming for a weekend, or want to get to know the city better, these two- and four-day itineraries will help you make the most of your visit.

Two Days in Barcelona

Day ❶
MORNING
Stroll along Barcelona's most celebrated avenue, **La Rambla** *(see pp16–17)*, then dive into the warren of medieval streets that makes up the **Barri Gòtic** *(see pp76–9)* and visit **Barcelona Cathedral** *(see pp18–19)*.

AFTERNOON
Continue your exploration of Barcelona's historic heart with a wander around the Born neighbourhood. Visit the **Museu Picasso** *(see pp30–31)*, then see if you can get tickets for an evening performance at the lavish Modernista **Palau de la Música Catalana** *(see pp32–3)*.

Day ❷
MORNING
Spend the morning marvelling at Gaudí's incredible **Sagrada Família** *(see pp12–15)*, but make sure you've booked tickets online in advance to avoid the long queues.

AFTERNOON
Ride the funicular up the green hill of Montjuïc *(see pp94–7)* to the **Fundació Joan Miró** *(see pp28–9)*, a stunning modern building that is home to a spectacular collection of Miró's work.

Four Days in Barcelona

Day ❶
MORNING
Make the day's first stop the playful, whimsical **Park Güell** *(see pp22–3)*, a UNESCO World Heritage Site.

AFTERNOON
Head south to the city's most iconic building, the **Sagrada Família** *(see pp12–15)*, then continue down to the

The vibrant Mercat de la Boqueria is one of Europe's largest markets for fresh produce, cheese and meat.

colourful **Els Encants** flea market *(see p108)*. After a bit of retail therapy, drop into the wonderful **Museu del Disseny** *(see p109)* to catch an exhibition.

Day ❷
MORNING
Take a stroll along **La Rambla** *(see pp16–17)*, ducking into the **Mercat de la Boqueria** *(see p68)* to admire the dizzying range of produce. Then meander through the medieval lanes of the **Barri Gòtic** *(see pp76–9)* to find **Barcelona Cathedral** *(see pp18–19)*.

AFTERNOON
Take in the boutiques of the elegant **Passeig de Gràcia** *(see p66)*, then visit one of Gaudí's most remarkable buildings, **La Pedrera** *(see pp26–7)*. Here you'll visit a restored apartment and the famous undulating rooftop.

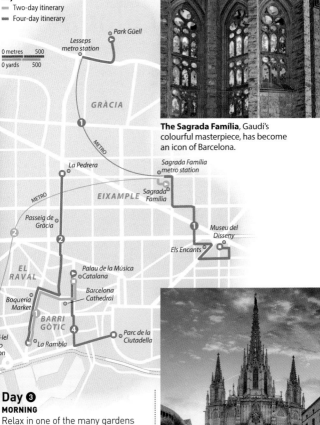

Key
— Two-day itinerary
— Four-day itinerary

0 metres 500
0 yards 500

GRÀCIA

Lesseps
metro station

Park Güell

METRO

La Pedrera

Sagrada Família
metro station

EIXAMPLE

Sagrada
Família

METRO

Passeig de
Gràcia

Museu del
Disseny

Els Encants

EL
RAVAL

Palau de la Música
Catalana

Barcelona
Cathedral

Boqueria
Market

BARRI
GÒTIC

Parc de la
Ciutadella

La Rambla

The Sagrada Família, Gaudí's
colourful masterpiece, has become
an icon of Barcelona.

**Barcelona's 13th-century
cathedral** has a magnificent
façade and a quiet cloister.

Day ❸
MORNING
Relax in one of the many gardens
on **Montjuïc** (see pp94–7), perhaps the
Jardins Laribel or **Jardins de Miramar**
(see p98), before visiting the **Fundació
Joan Miró** (see pp28–9), one of the
world's largest Miró collections.
AFTERNOON
You'd need more than an afternoon
to see every gallery at the **Museu
Nacional d'Art de Catalunya** (see
pp20–21), but the Romanesque and
Gothic collections are a must. In the
evening, enjoy the sound and light
show at the **Font Màgica** (see p95).

Day ❹
MORNING
Take a tour of the **Palau de la Música
Catalana** (see pp32–3), a breathtaking

Modernista masterpiece with
an eye-popping auditorium.
AFTERNOON
Amble over to the **Parc de la
Ciutadella** (see p101) and enjoy a
leisurely stroll through the city's
favourite park. Admire the spectacular Cascada fountain and hire a
rowboat for a punt around the lake.

Top 10 Barcelona Highlights

The soaring, tree-like columns
of the Sagrada Família's nave

 **Barcelona Highlights**

One of the busiest ports of the Mediterranean, Barcelona has it all. With beautiful Modernista buildings, atmospheric medieval streets, enchanting squares, beaches and treasure-filled museums, this awe-inspiring city will keep you coming back for more.

Sagrada Família ①

Gaudí's otherworldly *pièce de résistance* is the enduring symbol of the city and its Modernista legacy. Of the 18 planned spires, nine jut into the sky *(see pp12–15)*.

② La Rambla

Barcelona's centrepiece, this thriving pedestrian thoroughfare cuts a wide swathe through the old town, from Plaça de Catalunya to the glittering Mediterranean Sea *(see pp16–17)*.

③ Barcelona Cathedral

Dominating the heart of the old town is this magnificent Gothic cathedral, with a soaring, elaborate façade and a graceful, sun-dappled cloister containing palm trees and white geese *(see pp18–19)*.

Museu Nacional d'Art de Catalunya ④

The stately Palau Nacional is home to the Museu Nacional d'Art de Catalunya (MNAC). Its extensive collections feature some of the world's finest Romanesque art, rescued from churches around Catalonia during the 1920s *(see pp20–21)*.

⑤ Park Güell

With its whimsical dragon, fairy-tale pavilions and sinuous bench offering dramatic city views, this magical hillside park is indubitably the work of Gaudí *(see pp22–3)*.

6 La Pedrera

Unmistakably Gaudí, this Modernista marvel seems to grow from the very pavement itself. Its curving façade is fluid and alive, and mosaic chimneys keep watch over the rooftop like shrewd-eyed knights *(see pp26–7)*.

7 Fundació Joan Miró

An incomparable blend of art and architecture, this museum showcases the work of Joan Miró, one of Catalonia's greatest 20th-century artists. Paintings, sculptures, drawings and textiles represent 60 prolific years *(see pp28–9)*.

8 Museu Picasso

Housed in a medieval palace complex, this museum charts Picasso's rise to fame through an extensive collection of his early works, including many masterful portraits that he painted at the young age of 13 *(see pp30–31)*.

Palau de la Música Catalana 9

No mere concert hall, the aptly-named Palace of Catalan Music is one of the finest, and most exemplary, Modernista buildings in Barcelona *(see pp32–3)*.

10 Museu d'Art Contemporani and Centre de Cultura Contemporània

The city's gleaming contemporary art museum and its cutting-edge cultural centre have sparked an urban revival in the El Raval area *(see pp34–5)*.

🔟 ⭐ Sagrada Família

Nothing prepares you for the impact of the Sagrada Família. A *tour de force* of the imagination, Antoni Gaudí's church has provoked endless controversy. It also offers visitors the unique chance to watch a wonder of the world in the making. Over the last 90 years, at incalculable cost, sculptors and architects have continued to build Gaudí's dream. It was hoped the project would be complete by 2026, the 100th anniversary of Gaudí's death, however the pandemic in 2020 has delayed work.

1 Spiral Staircases
These helicoidal stone stairways **(above)**, which wind up the bell towers, look like snail shells.

2 Nave
The immense central body of the church **(below)**, now complete, is made up of leaning, tree-like columns with branches that are inspired by a banana tree spreading out across the ceiling; the overall effect is that of a beautiful stone forest.

3 Nativity Façade
Gaudí's love of nature is visible in this façade **(above)**. Up to 100 plant and animal species are sculpted in stone, and the two main columns are supported by turtles.

4 Apse
Adorned with serpents, four large snails and lizards, this was the first section to be completed by Gaudí. Here, the stained glass graduates in tones beautifully.

5 Hanging Model

This contraption is testimony to Gaudí's ingenuity. He made the 3D device – using multiple chains and tiny weighted sacks of lead pellets – as a model for the arches and vaulted ceilings of the Colonia Güell crypt. No one in the history of architecture had ever designed a building like this.

6 Spires

Gaudí's plan originally detailed a total of 18 spires. For a closer look at the mosaic tiling and gargoyles on the existing spires, take the lift up inside the bell tower. The views are equally spectacular.

7 Rosario's Claustro

In the only cloister to be finished by Gaudí, the imagery is thought to be inspired by the anarchist riots that began in 1909 (see pp38–9). The Devil's temptation of man is depicted by the sculpture of a serpent wound around a rebel.

Sagrada Família Floorplan

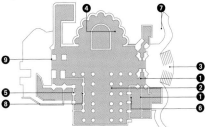

8 Crypt Museum

Gaudí now lies in the crypt (below), and his tomb is visible from the museum. Using audio-visual exhibits, the museum provides a lot of information about the construction of the church. The highlight is the maquette workshop, producing scale models for the ongoing work.

9 Passion Façade

Created between 1954 and 2002, this Josep Subirachs façade represents the sacrifice and pain of Jesus. The difference between the Gothic feel of Subirachs' style and the intricacy of Gaudí's work has been controversial.

10 Unfinished Business

The church buzzes with activity even today. You will see sculptors dangle from spires, stonemasons carve huge slabs of stone and cranes and scaffolding litter the site. Watching the construction in progress allows visitors to grasp the monumental scale of the project.

NEED TO KNOW

MAP G2 Entrances: C/Marina (for groups only) and C/Sardenya ■ 93 207 30 31 ■ www. sagradafamilia.org

Open 9am–6pm daily (Mar & Oct: to 7pm, Apr–Sep: to 8pm)

Adm €26 for basilica, including audio guide; €36 for basilica and towers, including audio guide; €30 for combined ticket with

Casa-Museu Gaudí, including audio guide

■ Advance online booking is strongly recommended. Check website for full details of guided tours.

■ Sit in a terrace bar on Av Gaudí and drink in the view of Gaudí's masterpiece illuminated at night.

■ For the best photos, get here before 8am: the light on the Nativity Façade is excellent and the tour buses haven't yet arrived.

Sight Guide

The main entrance is on C/Marina, in front of the Nativity Façade, along with gift shops. There is a lift in each façade (stairs are not open to the public). The museum is near the entrance on C/Sardenya. 12 of the 18 planned towers are built and are open to the public, but these are not accessible for those with specific requirements.

Key Sagrada Família Dates

1 1882
The first stone of the Sagrada Família is officially laid, with architect Francesc del Villar heading the project. Villar soon resigns after disagreements with the church's religious founders.

2 1883
The young, up-and-coming Antoni Gaudí is commissioned as the principal architect. He goes on to devote the next 40 years of his life to the project: by the end he even lives on the premises.

3 1889
The church crypt is completed, ringed by a series of chapels, one of which is later to house Gaudí's tomb.

4 1904
The final touches are made to the Nativity Façade, which depicts Jesus, Mary and Joseph amid a chorus of angels.

5 1925
The first of the 18 planned bell towers, measuring 100 m (328 ft) in height, is finished.

6 1926
On 10 June, Gaudí is killed by a tram while crossing the street near his beloved church. No one recognizes the city's most famous architect.

Sculpture, Passion Façade

7 1936
The military uprising and the advent of the Spanish Civil War brings construction of the Sagrada Família to a halt for some 20 years. During this period, Gaudí's studio and the crypt in the Sagrada Família are burned by revolutionaries, who despise the Catholic church for siding with the nationalists.

8 1987–1990
Sculptor and painter Josep Maria Subirachs (b.1927) takes to living in the Sagrada Família just as his famous predecessor did. Subirachs completes the statuary of the Passion Façade. His angular, severe and striking sculptures draw both criticism and praise.

9 2000
On 31 December, the nave is at long last declared complete.

10 2010–2021
The central nave of the church is complete, and in November 2010 Pope Benedict XVI consecrated it as a basilica. The Lion of Judah, among other things, was added to the Passion Façade in 2018, marking its completion. The construction, as Gaudí intended, continues today and relies on public subscriptions. The basilica's second-tallest tower, the tower of the Virgin Mary, is stunning up close.

Stained-glass windows in the apse

ANTONI GAUDÍ

Gaudí (1852–1926)

A flag bearer for the Modernista movement of the late 19th century, Antoni Gaudí is Barcelona's most famous architect. A strong Catalan nationalist and a devout Catholic, he led an almost monastic life, consumed by his architectural vision and living in virtual poverty for most of his life. In 2003 the Vatican opened the beatification process for Gaudí, which is the first step towards declaring his sainthood. Gaudí's extraordinary legacy dominates the architectural map of Barcelona. His name itself comes from the Catalan verb *gaudir*, meaning "to enjoy", and an enormous sense of exuberance and playfulness pervades his work. As was characteristic of *Modernisme*, nature prevails, not only in the decorative motifs, but also in the very structure of Gaudí's buildings. His highly innovative style is also characterized by intricate wrought-iron gates and balconies and *trencadís* tiling.

TOP 10
GAUDÍ SIGHTS IN BARCELONA

1 **Sagrada Família**

2 **La Pedrera** (1910)
see pp26–7

3 **Park Güell** (1900)
see pp22–3

4 **Casa Batlló** (1905)
see p45

5 **Palau Güell** (1890)
see p87

6 **Torre Bellesguard** (1875)

7 **Finca Güell** (1887)

8 **Casa Calvet** (1899)

9 **Col·legi de les Teresianes** (1890)

10 **Casa Vicens** (1885)

Casa Batlló's many chimneys are adorned with tiled designs. These usually unremarkable parts of a building have become notable examples of Gaudí's caprice.

La Rambla

One of the city's best-loved sights, the historic La Rambla avenue splits the Old Town in half as it stretches from Plaça de Catalunya to Port Vell. Lined with a host of enticing shops, charming cafés and tiny tapas bars, and teeming with locals, tourists and performance artists, this far-reaching street has long been a lively hub of exuberant activity. There may be no better place in the country to indulge in the Spanish ritual of the *paseo* (stroll) than on this wide, tree-shaded pedestrian street that snakes through the heart of the city.

1 Gran Teatre del Liceu

The city's grand opera house, founded in 1847, brought Catalan opera stars such as Montserrat Caballé to the world. Twice gutted by fire, it *(see p54)* has been fully restored.

2 Flower Stalls

La Rambla is teeming with life and things to distract the eye, but the true Rambla stalwarts are the flower stalls **(above)** flanking the pedestrian walkway, many run by the same families for decades.

3 Arts Santa Mònica

Once the haunt of rosary beads and prayers, this former 17th-century monastery was reborn in the 1980s as a contemporary art centre, thanks to government funding. This 'Centre de la Creativitat' lays special emphasis on encouraging creativity in Catalunya and promoting homegrown talent. Exhibitions here range from large-scale video installations to photography.

Visitors on La Rambla

4 Mercat de la Boqueria

A cacophonous shrine to food, this cavernous market *(see p68)* has it all, from stacks of fruit to suckling pigs and fresh lobsters.

5 Monument a Colom

Pointing resolutely out to sea, this 1888 bronze statue *(see p102)* of Christopher Columbus commemorates his return to Spain after his famed journey to the Americas. An elevator whisks visitors to the top of the column for stunning views.

6 Font de Canaletes

Ensure that you come back to the city by sipping water from this 19th-century fountain **(below)**. According to local legend, those who drink from it "will fall in love with Barcelona and always return".

7 Palau de la Virreina

This Neo-Classical palace was built by the viceroy of Peru in 1778. Today, the Palace of the Viceroy's Wife is home to the Centre de la Imatge, and hosts art exhibitions and cultural events.

8 Miró Mosaic

On the walkway on La Rambla is a colourful floor mosaic *(see p71)* by Catalan artist Joan Miró. Symbolizing the cosmos, it incorporates his signature abstract shapes and primary colours which unfold at your feet.

La Rambla

NEED TO KNOW

Gran Teatre del Liceu:
MAP L4; La Rambla 51–59; 93 485 99 31; www.liceubarcelona.cat

Mercat de La Boqueria:
MAP L3; La Rambla 91; open 8am–8:30pm Mon–Sat; www.boqueria. barcelona

Arts Santa Mònica:
MAP L5; La Rambla 7; 93 567 11 10; open 11am–9pm Tue–Sun; https://artssantamonica.gencat.cat/ca

Palau de la Virreina:
MAP L3; 93 316 10 00; La Rambla 99: open 11am–8pm Tue–Sun;

https://ajuntament. barcelona.cat/lavirreina/en

Església de Betlem:
MAP L3; C/Xuclà 2; 93 318 38 23; open 8:30am–1:30pm & 6–9pm daily; www.mdbetlem.com

■ Kick back at the Cafè de l'Òpera at No. 74 *(see p64)* and soak up the La Rambla ambience with a cool *granissat* (crushed ice drink) in hand.

■ La Rambla is rife with pickpockets – be careful with your belongings, especially your wallets and cameras.

9 Bruno Quadras Building

Once an umbrella factory, this late 19th-century building is decorated with Chinese-inspired motifs. Its exterior is festooned with umbrellas and an ornate Chinese Dragon statue **(above)**.

10 Església de Betlem

From a time when the Catholic Church was rolling in pesetas (and power), this hulking 17th-century church *(see p41)* is a seminal reminder of when La Rambla was more religious than risqué.

🔟 ⭐ Barcelona Cathedral

From its Gothic cloister and Baroque chapels to its splendid 19th-century façade, the cathedral, dating from 1298, is an amalgam of architectural styles, each one paying homage to a period in Spain's religious history. Records show that an early Christian baptistry was established here in the 6th century, later replaced by a Romanesque basilica in the 11th century, which gave way to the current Gothic cathedral. This living monument still functions as the Barri Gòtic's spiritual hub.

1 Main Façade
The 19th-century façade **(below)** has the entrance, flanked by twin towers, Modernista stained-glass windows and 100 carved angels. The restoration process took 8 years and was completed in 2011.

2 Choir Stalls
The lavish choir stalls (1340), crowned with wooden spires, are decorated with colourful coats of arms by artist Joan de Borgonya.

4 Nave and Organ
The immense nave **(above)** is supported by slender columns and features a raised high altar. The 16th-century organ looming over the interior fills the space with music during services.

3 Cloister
Graced with a fountain, palm trees and roaming geese, the cloister dates back to the 14th century. The mossy fountain is presided over by a small iron statue of Sant Jordi – St George *(see p41).*

Crypt of Santa Eulàlia 5
In the centre of the crypt lies the graceful 1327 alabaster sarcophagus **(right)** of Santa Eulàlia, Barcelona's first patron saint. Reliefs depict her martyrdom.

6 Capella de Sant Benet
Honouring Sant Benet, the patron saint of Europe, this chapel showcases the 15th-century altarpiece *Transfiguration of the Lord* by illustrious Catalan artist Bernat Martorell.

7 Capella de Santa Llúcia
This lovely Romanesque chapel is dedicated to Santa Llúcia, the patron saint of eyes and vision *(see p41)*. On her saint's day (13 December), the blind come to pray at her chapel.

Barcelona Cathedral Floorplan

8 Capella del Santíssim i Crist de Lepant
This 15th-century chapel features the Crist de Lepant **(right)** which, legend has it, guided the Christian fleet in the 16th-century Battle of Lepanto against the Ottoman Turks, who could not then advance to Europe.

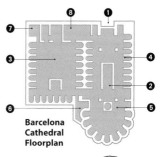

9 Pia Almoina and Museu Diocesà
The 11th-century Pia Almoina, once a rest house for pilgrims and the poor, houses the Museu Diocesà, which contains some of the cathedral's finest paintings, sculptures, fabrics and numismatics.

10 Casa de l'Ardiaca
Originally built in the 12th century, the Archdeacon's House is located near what was once the Bishop's Gate in the city's Roman walls. Expanded over the centuries, it now includes a lovely leafy patio with a fountain.

NEED TO KNOW

MAP M3 ■ Pl de la Seu; 93 342 82 62 ■ Open 10:30am–2pm & 4–7pm Mon–Fri, 10:30am–5:30pm Sat ■ Adm choir and rooftops (via lift) €3 each, for cathedral floor & cloister €7 donation (check website for timings) ■ www.catedralbcn.org

Museu Diocesà:
MAP N3; Av de la Catedral 4; open 10am–8pm daily (from 11am Tue); adm €8

Casa de l'Ardiaca:
MAP M3; C/Santa Llúcia 1; open 10am–2pm & 3–7:30pm Mon–Fri, by appointment

■ **Dress modestly to visit the cathedral** (covered shoulders; no shorts).

■ **Choral/organ concerts** are usually held monthly; check website for details.

■ **Watch** *Sardanes,* Catalonia's regional dance, performed in Plaça de la Seu at 6pm on Saturdays and at noon on Sundays.

Cathedral Guide
The main entrance is the main portal on Plaça de la Seu. As you enter, to the left you will find a series of chapels, the organ and elevators that go up to the roof. The Museu Diocesà is located to the left of the main entrance; Casa de l'Ardiaca is to the right.

TOP10 ⭐ Museu Nacional d'Art de Catalunya

Holding one of the most important medieval art collections in the world, the Museu Nacional d'Art de Catalunya (MNAC) is housed in the majestic Palau Nacional, built in 1929. A highlight is the Romanesque art section, which consists of the painted interiors of Pyrenean churches dating from the 11th and 12th centuries. Other collections include works by Catalan artists from the early 19th century to the present day.

① The Madonna of the Councillors

Commissioned by the city council in 1443, this work by Lluís Dalmau is rich in political symbolism, with the head councillors, saints and martyrs kneeling before an enthroned Virgin.

② Murals: Santa Maria de Taüll

The well-preserved interior of Santa Maria de Taüll (c.1123) gives an idea of how colourful the Romanesque churches must have been. There are scenes from Jesus's early life, with John the Baptist and the Wise Men.

③ Cambó Bequest

Catalan politician Francesc Cambó (1876–1974) left his huge art collection to Catalonia; two large galleries contain works from the 16th to early 19th centuries, including Tiepolo's 1756 *The Minuet* (above).

④ Thyssen-Bornemisza Collection

A small but fine selection from Baron Thyssen-Bornemisza's extensive collection. Among the magnificent paintings are Fra Angelico's sublime *Madonna of Humility* (1433–5) and a charmingly domestic *Madonna and Child* (c.1618) by Rubens (left).

⑤ Frescoes: Sant Climent de Taüll

The interior of Sant Climent de Taüll is a melange of French, Byzantine and Italian influences. The apse is dominated by *Christ in Majesty* (below) and the symbols of the four Evangelists and the Virgin with the apostles beneath.

7 Woman with Hat and Fur Collar

Picasso's extraordinary depiction of his lover Maria-Thérèse Walter shows him moving beyond Cubism and Surrealism into a new personal language, soon to be known simply as the "Picasso style".

9 Confidant from the Batlló House

Among the fine Modernista furnishings are some exquisite pieces by Antoni Gaudí, including an undulating wooden chair designed to encourage confidences between friends.

6 Ramon Casas and Pere Romeu on a Tandem

This painting **(above)** depicts the painter Casas and his friend Romeu, with whom he began the Barri Gòtic tavern Els Quatre Gats.

8 Crucifix of Batlló Majesty

This mid-12th century wooden carving is a depiction of Christ on the cross with open eyes and no signs of suffering, as he has defeated death.

10 Numismatics

The public numismatic collection at the MNAC dates back to the 6th century BC and features medals, early paper money, 15th-century Italian bills as well as coins **(above)** including the ones from the Greek colony of Empúries which had its own mint from the 5th century BC.

Museu Nacional d'Art de Catalunya Floorplan

- 10 Numismatics
- 6 Ramon Casas and Pere Romeu on a Tandem
- 4 Thyssen-Bornemisza Collection
- 3 Cambó Bequest
- 9 Confidant from the Batlló House
- 7 Woman with Hat and Fur Collar
- 2 Murals: Santa Maria de Taüll
- 1 The Madonna of the Councillors
- 5 Frescoes: Sant Climent de Taüll
- 8 Crucifix of Batlló Majesty

Key to Floorplan

- Romanesque Art Gallery
- Modern Art; Drawings, Prints and Posters
- Gothic Art Gallery
- Renaissance and Baroque Art
- Library

NEED TO KNOW

MAP B4 ■ Palau Nacional, Parc de Montjuïc ■ www.museunacional.cat/en

Open 10am–6pm Tue–Sat (May–Sep: to 8pm), 10am–3pm Sun; timings for roof terrace vary, check website.

Adm €12 (valid for 2 days in a month); free on Sat from 3pm and first Sun of the month; free for under 16s & over 65s; roof terrace €2

The museum has a busy programme of talks, screenings and workshops (usually in Spanish and Catalan only).

■ The terrace outside the front entrance of the museum has panoramic views over the city.

Gallery Guide

The Cambó Bequest, with Zurbarán's and Goya's works, and the Thyssen-Bornemisza Collection, with works from the Gothic to the Rococo, are on the ground floor, as are the Romanesque works. On the first floor are the modern art galleries and the photography and numismatics collections.

TOP 10 ⭐ Park Güell

Built between 1900 and 1914, Park Güell was conceived as an English-style garden city, which were becoming popular in the early 20th century. Gaudí's patron, Eusebi Güell, envisaged elegant, artistic villas, gardens and public spaces. However, the project failed. The space was sold to the city and, in 1926, reopened as a public park where Gaudí had let his imagination run riot on the pavilions, stairways, the main square with its sinuous tiled bench and the tiled columns of the marketplace.

Casa del Guarda ④

The porter's lodge, one of two fairy-tale pavilions that guard the park entrance (right), is now an outpost of MUHBA, the Barcelona History Museum *(see p78)*. It contains an exhibition dedicated to the history of Park Güell.

① Sala Hipòstila

Jujol was one of Gaudí's most gifted collaborators, responsible for decorating the 84 columns (above) of the park's marketplace, creating vivid ceiling mosaics from shards of broken tiles.

② Tiled Bench

An enormous bench, which functions as a balustrade, ripples around the edge of Plaça de la Natura. Artists ranging from Miró to Dalí were inspired by its beautiful abstract designs created from colourful broken tiles.

③ Jardins d'Àustria

These beautifully manicured gardens are modern, laid out in the 1970s on what was originally destined to be a plot for a mansion. They are especially lovely in the spring.

⑤ L'Escalinata del Drac

A fountain runs along the length of this impressive, lavishly-tiled staircase, which is topped with whimsical creatures. The most famous of these is the enormous multicoloured dragon, which has become a symbol of Barcelona.

⑥ Viaducts

Gaudí created three viaducts (below) to serve as carriageways through Park Güell. Set into the steep slopes, and supported by archways and columns in the shape of waves or trees, they appear to emerge organically from the hill.

⑦ Plaça de la Natura

The park's main square offers panoramic views across the city, and is fringed by a remarkable tiled bench. The square was originally called the Greek Theatre and was intended for open-air shows, with the audience watching from the surrounding terraces.

9 Pòrtic de la Bugadera

One of the park's many pathways, this is known as the Portico of the Laundress after the woman bearing a basket of washing on her head **(left)**, which is carved into an arch.

Park Güell

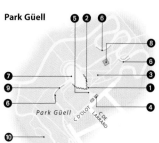

UNFULFILLED IDEAS

Sadly, many of Gaudí's ideas for Park Güell were never realized owing to the economic failure of Eusebi Güell's garden city. Among the most daring of these ideas was his design for an enormous entrance gate, which he intended to be swung open by a pair of gigantic mechanical gazelles.

10 Turó de les Tres Creus

Three crosses crown the very top of the hill, marking the spot where Gaudí and Güell, both intensely religious men, intended to build Park Güell's chapel. The climb to the top is well worth it in order to enjoy the spectacular city views.

8 Casa-Museu Gaudí

One of only two houses to be built in Park Güell, this became Gaudí's home and contains original furnishings and memorabilia. It is located outside the Monumental Zone.

NEED TO KNOW

MAP C1 ■ C/d'Olot s/n ■ https://parkguell.barcelona

Open Mid-Feb–mid-Mar: 9:30am–6pm daily; mid-Mar–mid-Oct: 9:30am–7:30pm daily; Nov–mid-Feb: 9:30am–5:30pm daily

Adm to Monumental Zone €10; free for under 6s, €7 under 12s; the rest of the park is free of charge; Casa del Guarda included with park ticket; separate ticket required in advance for Casa-Museu Gaudí, open Sat & Sun, adm €6

■ There are very few options to eat around the Park Güell, so it's a good idea to bring a picnic.

There are a couple of picnic areas with tables available.

■ Note that visits to the Monumental Area are timed. Ensure that you do not miss your slot as the schedules are not flexible.

■ There are three small playgrounds with swings and slides, perfect to let little ones blow off some steam.

Following pages Elegant Neo-Classical buildings and towering palm trees on Plaça Reial

TOP 10 ⭐ La Pedrera

Completed in 1912, this fantastic, undulating apartment block with its out-of-this-world roof is one of the most emblematic of all Gaudí's works. Casa Milà, also known as La Pedrera ("the stone quarry"), was Gaudí's last great civic work before he dedicated himself to the Sagrada Família. What makes it so magical is that every detail bears the hallmark of Gaudí's visionary genius. Now restored to its former glory, La Pedrera contains the Espai Gaudí, an exhibition hall, courtyards, a roof terrace and the Pedrera Apartment.

1 **Façade and Balconies**
Defying the laws of gravity, La Pedrera's irreverent curved walls are held in place by undulating horizontal beams attached to invisible girders. Intricate wrought-iron balconies **(below)** are an example of the artisan skill so integral to *Modernisme*.

4 **Roof**
The strikingly surreal rooftop sculpture park has chimneys resembling medieval warriors and huge ventilator ducts twisted into bizarre organic forms **(below)**, not to mention superb views over the Eixample.

2 **Espai Gaudí**
A series of drawings, photos, maquettes and multimedia displays help visitors grasp Gaudí's architectural wizardry. The museum is housed in the breathtaking vaulted attic, with its 270 catenary brick arches forming atmospheric skeletal corridors.

6 **Temporary Exhibition Hall**
This interesting gallery space is run by the Catalunya-La Pedrera Foundation and hosts regular free art exhibitions. It has displayed works by Francis Bacon, Salvador Dalí and Marc Chagall among others. The ceiling here looks as if it has been coated with whisked egg whites.

3 **Interior Courtyard: Carrer Provença**
A brigade of guides take the multitude of visitors through here each day. A closer inspection of this first courtyard reveals its beautiful mosaics and multicoloured wall paintings lining a swirling, fairy-tale staircase.

5 **Gates**
The mastery in imagining the huge wrought-iron gates **(right)** reveals the influence of Gaudí's predecessors – four generations of artisan metal workers. The use of iron is integral to many of Gaudí's edifices.

8 La Pedrera Apartment

This Modernista flat **(left)** with period furnishings is a reconstruction of a typical Barcelona bourgeois flat of the late 19th century. It provides an engaging contrast between the more sedate middle-class conservatism of the era and the undeniable wackiness of the outer building itself.

Visitors exploring the unusual roof of La Pedrera

7 Interior Courtyard: Passeig de Gràcia

Like the first courtyard, this too has a grand, ornate staircase **(below)**. This one is decorated with a stunning, floral ceiling painting.

9 Auditorium

The auditorium, located in the former coach house, hosts regular events such as jazz and contemporary concerts. The adjacent garden offers visitors a glimpse of greenery.

NEED TO KNOW

MAP E2 ◼ Pg de Gràcia 92 ◼ 93 214 2576 ◼ www.la pedrera.com

Open 9am–8:30pm daily (Nov–Feb : to 6:30pm, 8:30pm at Christmas time); times for evening guided tours and temporary exhibits vary

Adm €28 (€25 online); audio guides in several languages included; reserve ahead

◼ Check the website for current activities and temporary exhibitions.

◼ Explore La Pedrera with nocturnal and early morning tours, or opt for a combined guided tour where you can experience the sight day and night.

◼ Tickets for the popular night-time sound and light show can be booked online for €35.

Sight Guide
The Espai Gaudí, the Pedrera Apartment, the Passeig de Gràcia and Carrer Provença Courtyards, the Exhibition Room and the roof are open to visitors. A lift goes up to the apartment, Espai Gaudí and the roof. The courtyards, staircases, café and shop are accessible from the entrance on the corner of Pg de Gràcia and C/Provença.

10 La Pedrera Shop and Café

A wide range of Gaudí-related memorabilia includes replicas of the warrior chimneys in ceramic and bronze.

🔟 ⭐ Fundació Joan Miró

Founded in 1975 by Joan Miró himself, who wanted it to be a contemporary arts centre, this is now a superb tribute to a man whose legacy as an artist and a Catalan is visible across the city. The museum holds more than 14,000 of his paintings, sketches and sculptures, tracing Miró's evolution from an innovative Surrealist in the 1920s to one of the world's most challenging modern artists in the 1960s.

① Tapis de la Fundació

This immense, richly coloured tapestry (below) represents the culmination of Miró's work with textiles, which began during the 1970s. The work framed the characteristic colour palette of Miró's output.

The façade of Fundació Joan Miró

③ L'Estel Matinal

This is one of 23 paintings known as the Constellation Series. The *Morning Star*'s intro-spective quality reflects Miró's state of mind at the outbreak of World War II, when he was hiding in Normandy. Spindly shapes of birds, women, heavenly bodies, lines and planes of colour are suspended in an undefined space.

② Pagès Català al Clar de Lluna

The figurative painting *Catalan Peasant by Moonlight* (right) dates from the late 1960s and highlights two of Miró's favourite themes: the earth and the night. The figure of the peasant, a simple collage of colour, is barely decipherable, as the crescent moon merges with his sickle and the night sky takes on the rich green tones of the earth.

④ Home i Dona Davant un Munt d'Excrements

Tortured and misshapen semi-abstract figures try to embrace against a black sky. Miró's pessi-mism at the time of *Man and Woman in Front of a Pile of Excrement* would soon be confirmed by the outbreak of the Civil War.

9 Terraces

More of Miró's sculptures are scattered on terraces **(left)**, from which you can appreciate the Rationalist architecture of Josep Lluís Sert's geometric building. The 3-m (10-ft) tall *Caress of a Bird* (1967) dominates the terrace.

7 Font de Mercuri

Alexander Calder donated the *Mercury Fountain* to the Fundació as a mark of his friendship with Miró. The work was an anti-fascist tribute, conceived in memory of the attack on the town of Almadén.

8 Espai 13

This space showcases the experimental work of new artists from around the world. The exhibitions, based on a single theme each year, are usually radical and often use new technologies.

10 Sculpture Room

This room **(below)** focuses on Miró's sculptures from the 1940s to the 1950s, when he experimented with ceramic, bronze and, later, painted media and found objects. Notable works include *Sun Bird* and *Moon Bird* (both 1946–9).

5 Sèrie Barcelona

The Fundació holds the only complete set of prints of this series of 50 black-and-white lithographs. This important collection is only occasionally on display.

6 Visiting Exhibitions

Over the years, a number of temporary exhibitions, which are usually held in the Fundació's west wing, have included retrospectives of high-profile artists such as Mark Rothko, Andy Warhol, René Magritte and Fernand Léger.

NEED TO KNOW

MAP B4 ▪ Av Miramar, Parc de Montjuïc ▪ 93 443 94 70 ▪ www.fmiro bcn.org

Open 10am–6pm Tue–Sun (Apr–Oct : to 8pm)

Adm €13, concessions €7; Espai 13 free; multimedia guide €5; temporary exhibitions €7

▪ The restaurant-café has a garden terrace with indoor and outdoor seating and is one of the area's best dining options.

▪ Regular activities including readings, screenings and concerts are held here; check the website for details.

▪ The gift shop has an original range of Miróesque curiosities, from tablecloths to champagne glasses.

Katsuta Collection

The Foundation's collections have been supplemented with 32 important artworks loaned out by Kazumasa Katsuta, a Japanese businessman who owns the world's largest private collection of Miró's works.

TOP 10 ⭐ Museu Picasso

Pay homage to the 20th century's most acclaimed artist at this treasure-filled museum. Highlighting Pablo Picasso's (1881–1973) formative years, the museum houses the world's largest collection of his early works. At the tender age of 10, Picasso was already revealing remarkable artistic tendencies. In 1895 he moved to Barcelona where he blossomed as an artist. From precocious sketches and powerful family portraits to Blue- and Rose-period works, the museum offers visitors the rare chance to discover the artist as he was discovering himself.

① Home amb boina
This portrait reveals brush strokes – and a subject matter – that are far beyond a 13-year-old child. No puppies or cats for the young Picasso; instead, he painted the portraits of the oldest men in the village. He signed this work P Ruiz, because at this time he was still using his father's last name.

④ L'Espera (Margot) and La Nana
Picasso's *Margot* is an evocative painting portraying a call girl as she waits for her next customer, while *La Nana* **(left)** captures the defiant expression and stance of a heavily rouged dwarf dancer.

⑤ El Foll
The Madman is a fine example of Picasso's Blue period. This artistic phase, which lasted from 1901 to 1904, was characterized by melancholic themes and monochromatic, sombre colours.

② Autoretrat amb perruca
At 14, Picasso painted *Self-portrait with Wig*, a whimsical depiction of how he might have looked during the time of his artistic hero, Velázquez.

③ Ciència i Caritat
One of Picasso's first publicly exhibited paintings was *Science and Charity*. Picasso's father posed as the doctor.

⑥ Menu de Els Quatre Gats
Picasso's premier Barcelona exhibition was held in 1900 at the Barri Gòtic café and centre of *Modernisme*, Els Quatre Gats. The artist's first commission was the pen-and-ink drawing **(left)** of himself and a group of artist friends, which graced the menu cover of this bohemian hang-out.

8 Arlequí

A lifting of spirits led to Picasso's Neo-Classical period, typified by paintings like *Arlequí* or *The Harlequin* **(left)**, which celebrated the light-hearted liberty of circus performers.

7 Las Meninas Series

Picasso's reverence for Velázquez culminated in this remarkable series of paintings **(below)**, based on the Velázquez painting *Las Meninas*.

9 Home assegnt

Works such as *Seated Man* **(above)** confirmed Picasso's status as the greatest Analytic Cubist painter of the 20th century.

10 Cavall banyegat

The anguished horse in this painting later appears in Picasso's large mural *Guernica*, which reveals the horrors of war. This work gives viewers the chance to observe the process that went into the creation of one of Picasso's most famous paintings.

NEED TO KNOW

MAP P4 ■ C/Montcada 15–23 ■ www.museu picasso.bcn.cat

Open 10am–7pm Tue–Sun

Adm €12; temporary exhibitions €7; free first Sunday of the month (permanent collections) and 4–7pm every Thursday

Guided tours in English are available at 3pm

and 4pm on Tuesday and at 11am on Sunday; adm €6 plus price of ticket

■ The Museu Picasso is housed in a Gothic palace complex, replete with leafy courtyards, all of which can be explored.

■ The café has outdoor tables in summer and offers a changing menu of daily lunch specials.

Gallery Guide

The museum is housed in five interconnected medieval palaces featuring stone archways and pretty courtyards. The permanent collection is arranged chronologically on the first and second floors of the first three palaces. The last two host temporary exhibitions on the first and second floors.

🔟 ⭐ Palau de la Música Catalana

Barcelona's Modernista movement reached its aesthetic peak in Lluís Domènech i Montaner's magnificent 1908 concert hall. The lavish façade is ringed by mosaic pillars, and each part of the foyer in Domènech's "garden of music", from banisters to pillars, has a floral motif. The concert hall, whose height is the same as its breadth, is a celebration of natural forms, capped by a stained-glass dome that floods the space with sunlight.

① Stained-Glass Ceiling
Topping the concert hall is a breathtaking, stained-glass inverted dome ceiling **(below)**. By day, sunlight streams through the fiery red and orange stained glass, illuminating the hall.

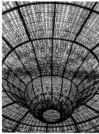

④ Stained-Glass Windows
Blurring the boundaries between the outdoors and the interior, the architect encircled this concert hall with vast stained-glass windows decorated with floral designs that let in sunlight and reveal the changing time of day.

② Rehearsal Hall of the Orfeó Català
This semicircular, acoustically sound rehearsal room is a smaller version of the massive concert hall one floor above. At its centre is an inlaid foundation stone that commemorates the construction of the Palau.

⑤ Horse Sculptures
Charging from the ceiling are sculptor Eusebi Aranu's winged horses, infusing the concert hall with movement and verve. Also depicted is a representation of Wagner's chariot ride of the Valkyries, led by galloping horses that leap towards the stage.

⑥ Façade
The towering façade **(above)** reveals Modernista delights on every level. An elaborate mosaic represents the Orfeó Català choral society, founded in 1891.

③ Stage
The semicircular stage **(right)** swarms with activity – even when no one's performing. Eighteen mosaic and terracotta muses spring from the backdrop, playing everything from the harp to the castanets.

7 Busts

A bust of Catalan composer Josep Anselm Clavé (1824–74) marks the Palau's commitment to Catalan music. Facing him across the concert hall, a stern, unruly-haired Beethoven **(left)** represents the hall's classical and international repertoire.

8 Foyer and Bar

Modernista architects worked with stone, wood, ceramic, marble and glass, all of which Domènech used liberally, most notably in the opulent foyer.

9 Lluís Millet Hall

Named after Catalan composer Lluís Millet, this immaculately-preserved lounge has gorgeous stained-glass windows. On the main balcony outside are rows of stunning mosaic pillars, each with a different design.

10 Concert and Dance Series

Over 500 concerts and dance shows are staged each year, and seeing a show here is a thrilling experience **(right)**. For symphonic concerts, keep an eye out for the Palau 100 Series; for choral concerts, look out for the Orfeó Català series.

NEED TO KNOW

MAP N2 ▪ Sant Pere Més Alt ▪ 90 247 54 85 ▪ www.palaumusica.cat

Guided tours and self-guided tours (with audio guides) 9:30am–3:30pm daily; advance booking recommended; mini recital available

Adm €16, €20 (guided visit €24); free for under 10s

▪ Café Palau offers free live music performances on its terrace. Check the website for details.

▪ The Palau shop sells items inspired by the building's architecture and it also has a section devoted to children.

▪ Buy tickets online, or from the box office *(open 9am–9pm Mon–Fri, 9:30am–9pm Sat, 9:30am–1pm Sun and 2 hrs before the concert).*

ORFEÓ CATALÀ

The famous choral group, Orfeó Català, for whom the concert hall was originally built, performs here regularly and holds a concert on 26 December every year. Book in advance.

🔟 ⭐ Museu d'Art Contemporani and Centre de Cultura Contemporània

Barcelona's sleek contemporary art museum stands in bold contrast to its surroundings. The Museu d'Art Contemporani (MACBA), together with the Centre de Cultura Contemporània (CCCB) nearby, has provided a focal point for the city since 1995 and has played an integral part in the rejuvenation of El Raval. MACBA's permanent collection includes big-name Spanish and international artists, while the CCCB serves as a cutting-edge exploration of contemporary culture.

Façade ①
American architect Richard Meier's stark, white, geometrical façade **(right)** makes a startling impression against the dull and industrial-toned backdrop of this working-class neighbourhood. On the front side, hundreds of panes of glass reflect the skateboarders who gather here daily.

② Visiting Artist's Space
The *raison d'être* of MACBA is this flexible area showing the best in contemporary art. Past exhibitions have included Zush and acclaimed painter Dieter Roth.

③ Revolving Permanent Collection
The permanent collection comprises more than 2,000 modern artworks, 10 per cent of which are on show at any one time. All major contemporary artist trends are represented. This 1974 work **(below)** by Eduardo Arranz Bravo is titled *Homea*.

④ Interior Corridors
Space and light are omnipresent in the museum's bare white walkways that hover between floors **(left)**. Look through the glass panels onto the Plaça dels Àngels for myriad images before you even enter the gallery spaces.

8 A Sudden Awakening

One of the only pieces of art on permanent display is Antoni Tàpies' deconstructed bed (1992–3), with its bedding flung across the wall in disarray **(left)**. Its presence to the right of the main entrance underlines the late Tàpies' importance in the world of Catalan modern art.

5 Capella MACBA

One of the few surviving Renaissance chapels in Barcelona has been converted for use as MACBA's temporary exhibition space *[see p87]*. It is located in a former convent across the Plaça dels Àngels.

9 Thinking and Reading Spaces

Pleasant and unusual features of MACBA are the white leather sofas between the galleries. Usually next to a shelf of relevant books and a set of headphones, these quiet spaces provide the perfect resting spot to contemplate – and learn more about – the art.

10 Temporary Exhibitions/ CCCB

Exhibitions at the CCCB tend to be more theme-based than artist-specific. It hosts the World Press Photo exhibition in spring and numerous literary festivals throughout the year. Home to several fascinating avant-garde art exhibits, the CCCB is always at the forefront of the latest cultural trends.

El Pati de les Dones/CCCB 6

This courtyard **(right)** off Carrer Montalegre forms part of the neighbouring CCCB. An ultramodern prismatic screen acts as a mirror reflecting the medieval courtyard, giving visitors a magical juxtaposition of different architectural styles.

7 Plaça Joan Coromines

The contrast between the modern MACBA, the University building, the Tuscan-style CCCB and the 19th-century mock-Romanesque church make this square one of the city's most enchanting. It is home to the terrace restaurants of MACBA and CCCB.

NEED TO KNOW

MACBA: **MAP K2**; Pl dels Àngels; 93 481 33 68; open 11am–7:30pm Mon & Wed–Fri, 10am–7:30pm Sat (to 3pm Sun); adm €11 (€10 online); concessions €8.80; free for under 14s; www.macba.cat/en

CCCB: **MAP K1**; C/ Montalegre 5; 93 306 41 00; open 11am–8pm Tue–Sun; adm €6 for 1 show, €8 for 2 shows; concessions €4 for 1 show, €6 for 2 shows; free for under 12s; free every Sunday 3–8pm; www.cccb.org

■ Pause at the nearby Doña Rosa café *(C/Ferlandina),* which offers a range of modern Mediterranean food to a hip crowd, or at CCCB's delightful Terracccita Bar.

■ MACBA offers tours in sign language as well as adapted tours for the visually impaired.

Sights Guide

Although they share the Plaça Joan Coromines, MACBA and CCCB have separate entrances. Both multilevel galleries have flexible display spaces. MACBA has rest areas dotted among the galleries on all floors, allowing you to take breaks as you explore.

The Top 10
of Everything

Art Nouveau façade of Casa Vicens, embellished with bright graphic tiles

🔟 Moments in History

1 3rd Century BC: The Founding of a City

Barcino, as the city was first known, was founded in the 3rd century BC by Carthaginian Hamilcar Barca. It was taken by the Romans in 218 BC but played second fiddle in the region to the provincial capital of Tarragona.

2 4th–11th Centuries: Early Invasions

As the Roman Empire began to fall apart in the 5th century, Visigoths from the Toulouse area took over the city. They were followed in the 8th century by the Moors, who moved up through the Iberian peninsula at great speed. Around AD 800, Charlemagne took over the area with the help of the Pyrenean counts, bringing it back under the control of the Franks.

Exhibition poster, 1929

3 12th–16th Centuries: The Middle Ages

During this period, Barcelona was the capital of a Catalan empire that stretched across the Mediterranean. The city's fortune was built on commerce, but as neighbouring Castile expanded into the New World, trading patterns shifted and the Catalan dynasty faltered. Barcelona fell into decline and came under Castilian domination.

4 1638–1652: Catalan Revolt

In reaction to the oppressive policies set out in Madrid, now ruled by the Austrian Habsburgs, various local factions, known as *Els Segadors*, rebelled. Fighting began in 1640 and dragged on until 1652, when the Catalans and their French allies were finally defeated.

5 19th Century: Industry and Prosperity

Booming industry and trade with the Americas brought activity to the city. Immigrants poured in from the countryside, laying the foundations of prosperity but also seeds of unrest. The old city walls came down, broad Eixample avenues were laid out and workers crowded into the old city neighbourhoods left behind by the middle classes.

6 1888–1929: The Renaixença

The International Exhibitions of 1888 and 1929 sparked a Catalan renaissance. Modernista mansions came up and the nationalists oversaw a revival of Catalan culture.

7 1909–1931: The Revolutionary Years

Discontent was brewing among workers, Catalan nationalists, communists, Spanish fascists, royalists, anarchists and republicans. In 1909, protests against the Moroccan war turned into a brutal riot, the *Setmana Tràgica* (Tragic Week). Lurching towards Civil War, Catalonia suffered under a dictatorship before being declared a republic in 1931.

8 1936–1975: Civil War and Franco

At the outbreak of war in 1936, Barcelona's workers and militants managed to fend off General Franco's troops for a while. The city was taken

y Fascist forces in 1939, prompting
a wave of repression, particularly of
the Catalan language, which was
banned in schools.

Franco addressing a rally, 1939

9 1975–1980s: Transition to Democracy

Franco's death in 1975 paved the way
for democracy. The Catalan language
was rehabilitated and the region was
granted autonomy. The first Catalan
government was elected in 1980.

10 1992–Present Day: The Olympics and Beyond

Barcelona was catapulted onto the
world stage in 1992 with the highly
successful Olympic Games. Calls for
Catalan independence grew stronger
over the years and a referendum was
held in 2017 but deemed illegal by
Spain; nine politicians were imprisoned. They were pardoned in 2021,
when the government agreed to talks.
The movement remains divided over
the best way to move forward.

Opening ceremony, 1992 Olympics

TOP 10 HISTORICAL FIGURES

Ferdinand the Catholic

1 Guifré the Hairy
The first Count of Barcelona (d.897),
seen as Catalonia's founding father.

2 Ramon Berenguer IV
He united Catalonia and joined it with
Aragon by marrying the Aragonese
princess Petronilla in 1137.

3 Jaume I of Aragon
This 13th-century warrior-king seized
control of the Balearics and Valencia,
laying the foundations for the empire.

4 Ramon Llull
Mallorcan philosopher and missionary,
Llull (d.1316) is the greatest figure in
medieval Catalan literature.

5 Ferdinand the Catholic
King of Aragon and Catalonia (d.1516),
he married Isabella of Castile, paving the
way for the formation of a united Spain
and the end of Catalan independence.

6 Francesca Bonnemaison
A supporter of women's education,
she established Europe's first women-
only library in Barcelona in 1909.

7 Antoni Gaudí
Gaudí was responsible for Barcelona's
most famous Modernista monuments.

8 Francesc Macià
This socialist nationalist politician
proclaimed the birth of the Catalan
Republic in 1931 and Catalan regional
autonomy in 1932.

9 Lluís Companys
Catalan president during the Civil War.
Exiled in France, he was arrested by
the Gestapo in 1940 and returned
to Franco, who had him executed.

10 Ada Colau
An activist turned politician, Colau is
now the mayor of Barcelona, famed for
her pedestrian-friendly superblocks.

TOP 10 Churches and Chapels

1 Barcelona Cathedral

Barcelona's magnificent Gothic cathedral (see pp18–19) has an eye-catching façade and a peaceful cloister.

2 Basilica de Santa Maria del Mar

The elegant church (see pp78–9) of Santa Maria del Mar (1329–83) is one of the finest examples of Catalan Gothic, a style characterized by simplicity. A spectacular stained-glass rose window illuminates the lofty interior.

Rose window, Església de Santa Maria del Mar

3 Temple Expiatori del Sagrat Cor

MAP B1 ■ Pl del Tibidabo ■ 93 417 56 86 ■ Open 11am–8:30pm daily ■ Adm for lifts

Mount Tibidabo is an appropriate perch for this over-the-top Neo-Gothic church (see p119), topped with a large golden statue of Christ with arms outstretched. The name Tibidabo comes from the words *tibidabo*, meaning "I shall give you", said to have been uttered by the Devil in his temptation of Christ. Zealously serving the devoted, the priest here celebrates the Eucharist throughout the day.

Temple Expiatori del Sagrat Cor

4 Església de Sant Pau del Camp

Founded as a Benedictine monastery in the 9th century by Guifre II, a count of Barcelona, this church (see p89) was rebuilt the following century. Its sculpted façade and intimate cloister with rounded arches exemplify the Romanesque style.

5 Església de Sant Pere de les Puel·les

MAP P2 ■ Pl de Sant Pere ■ Open for Mass: 7pm Mon–Fri, 5pm Sat, 11am & 12:30pm Sun

Built in 801 as a chapel for troops stationed in Barcelona, this *església* later became a spiritual retreat for young noblewomen. The church was rebuilt in the 1100s and is notable for its Romanesque central cupola and a series of capitals with carved leaves. Look out for two stone tablets depicting a Greek cross, which are from the original chapel.

6 Capella de Sant Miquel and Església al Monestir de Pedralbes

Accessed through an arch set in ancient walls, the lovely Monestir de Pedralbes (see p117), founded in 1327, still has the air of a closed community. Inside is a Gothic cloister and the Capella de Sant Miquel, decorated with murals by Catalan artist Ferrer Bassa in 1346. The adjoining Gothic church contains the alabaster tomb of Queen Elisenda, the monastery's founder. On the church side, her effigy wears royal robes and on the other, a nun's habit.

Basilica de Santa Maria del Pi

MAP L3 ■ Pl del Pi ■ Open 11am–6pm Mon–Sat ■ Adm

This lovely Gothic church with its ornate stained-glass windows graces the Plaça del Pi *(see p47)*. The rose window is one of the largest in Catalonia.

 Capella de Santa Àgata

MAP N3 ■ Pl del Rei ■ Open 10am–2pm & 3–8pm Tue–Sun ■ Adm (free 3–8pm Sun)

Within the beautiful Palau Reial is the medieval Capella de Santa Àgata, which can only be entered as part of a visit to the Museu d'Història de Barcelona *(see p78)*. The 15th-century altarpiece is by Jaume Huguet.

 Capella de Sant Jordi

MAP M4 ■ Pl Sant Jaume ■ Open 2nd and 4th weekend of month

In the Palau de la Generalitat *(see p77)* is this fine 15th-century chapel, dedicated to the patron saint of Catalonia.

Interior of the Església de Betlem

Església de Betlem

La Rambla *(see pp16–17)* was once dotted with religious buildings, most dating to the 17th and 18th centuries. This Baroque *església* is one of the major functioning churches from this period. Immensely popular around Christmas, it hosts one of the largest displays of *pessebres* (manger scenes) in the world.

The famous Virgin of Montserrat

TOP 10 CATALAN SAINTS AND VIRGINS

1 Virgin of Montserrat
The famous "Black Virgin" is a patron saint of Catalonia, along with Sant Jordi.

2 Sant Jordi
Catalonia's patron saint is St George, whose dragon-slaying prowess is depicted all over the city.

3 Virgin of Mercè
The Virgin of Mercè became a patron saint of the city in 1687, and shares the honour with Santa Eulàlia. Festes de la Mercè *(see p73)* is the most raucous festival in town.

4 Santa Eulàlia
Santa Eulàlia is Barcelona's co-patron saint (with La Mercè). She was martyred by the Romans in around AD 300.

5 Santa Elena
Legend has it that St Helena converted to Christianity after finding Christ's cross in Jerusalem in AD 346.

6 Santa Llúcia
The patron saint of eyes and vision is celebrated on 13 December, when the blind come to worship at the Santa Llúcia chapel in Barcelona Cathedral *(see pp18–19)*.

7 Sant Cristòfor
Cars are blessed on the feast day of Sant Cristòfor, patron saint of travellers, at a tiny chapel on C/Regomir *(see p80)*.

8 Sant Antoni de Padua
On 13 June, those seeking a husband or wife pray to the patron saint of love.

9 Santa Rita
Those searching for miracles pray to Santa Rita, deliverer of the impossible.

10 Sant Joan
The night of St John *(see p72)* is celebrated with bonfires and fireworks.

🔟 Museums and Galleries

The modern buildings of the Fundació Joan Miró

1 Fundació Joan Miró
The airy, high-ceilinged galleries of this splendid museum (see pp28–9) are a fitting home for the bold, abstract works of Joan Miró, one of Catalonia's most acclaimed 20th-century artists.

2 Museu Nacional d'Art de Catalunya
Discover Catalonia's Romanesque and Gothic heritage at this impressive museum (see pp20–21), housed in the 1929 Palau Nacional. Highlights include striking medieval frescoes and a collection of Modernista furnishings and artworks.

3 Museu Picasso
Witness the budding – and meteoric rise – of Picasso's artistic genius at this unique museum (see pp30–31), one of the world's largest collections of the painter's early works.

4 Museu d'Art Contemporani & Centre de Cultura Contemporània
Inaugurated in 1995, MACBA is Barcelona's centre for modern art. Combined with the neighbouring CCCB, the two buildings form an artistic and cultural hub in the heart of El Raval (see pp34–5).

Both regularly host temporary exhibitions: the MACBA showcases contemporary artists; the CCCB is more theme-based.

5 Fundació Tàpies
Works by Catalan artist Antoni Tàpies are showcased in this graceful Modernista building (see p108). Venture inside to discover Tàpies' rich repertoire, from early collage works to large abstract paintings, many alluding to political and social themes.

6 Museu d'Història de Barcelona (MUHBA)
Explore the medieval Palau Reial and wander among the splendid remains of Barcelona's Roman walls and waterways at the city's history museum. The museum is partly housed in the 15th-century Casa Padellàs on the impressive medieval Plaça del Rei.

FC Barcelona badge

7 Museu del FC Barcelona
This shrine to the city's football club houses trophies, posters and memorabilia that celebrate the club's 100-year history. The museum can only be visited in combination with a tour of the adjacent Camp Nou Stadium (see p118).

8 Museu Frederic Marès

Catalan sculptor Frederic Marès (1893–1991) was a passionate and eclectic collector. Housed here, under one roof, are many remarkable finds amassed during his travels (see p78). Among the vast array of historical objects on display are Romanesque and Gothic religious art and sculptures, plus everything from dolls and fans to pipes and walking sticks.

9 Museu Marítim

The formidable seafaring history of Barcelona is showcased in the cavernous, 13th-century Drassanes Reials (Royal Shipyards). The collection (see p87), which ranges from the Middle Ages to the 19th century, includes a full-scale replica of the *Real*, the flagship galley of Don Juan of Austria, who led the Christians to victory against the Turks at the Battle of Lepanto in 1571. Also on display are model ships, maps and navigational instruments.

Medieval warship, Museu Marítim

10 CosmoCaixa Museu de la Ciència

Exhibits covering the whole history of science, from the Big Bang to the computer age, are housed in this modern museum (see p118). Highlights include an interactive tour of the geological history of our planet, an area of real Amazonian rainforest, and a planetarium. There are also temporary displays on environmental issues and family activities.

TOP 10 QUIRKY MUSEUMS AND MONUMENTS

Wax models at the Museu de Cera

1 Museu de Cera
MAP L5 = Ptge de la Banca 7
Home to over 350 wax figures, from Marilyn Monroe to Franco and Gaudí.

2 Hash, Marihuana and Hemp Museum
MAP E5 = C/Ample 35
This cannabis museum is set in a magnificent Modernista building.

3 Casa dels Entremesos
MAP N3 = Pl Beates 2
Traditional Catalan puppets such as *gegants* (giants) and *capgrossos* (fatheads) are found here.

4 Moco Museum
MAP P4 = C/Montcada 25
This modern art museum features digital installations.

5 Museu dels Autòmates
MAP B1 = Parc d'Atraccions del Tibidabo
A colourful museum of human and animal automatons.

6 Museu de la Xocolata
MAP P4 = C/Comerç 36
A celebration of chocolate; enjoy interactive exhibits, edible city models and tastings.

7 Museu del Disseny
MAP H3 = Pl de les Glòries Catalanes
A design museum covering clothes, architecture, objects and graphic design.

8 Museu del Perfum
MAP E2 = Pg de Gràcia 39
The museum displays perfume bottles from Roman times to the present.

9 Cap de Barcelona
MAP N5 = Pg de Colom
Pop artist Roy Lichtenstein's "Barcelona Head", created for the 1992 Olympics.

10 Peix
MAP G5 = Port Olímpic
Frank Gehry's huge shimmering goldfish sculpture (1992).

🔟 Modernista Buildings

project (see p107) was planned around two avenues running at 45-degree angles to the Eixample streets. Started by Domènech i Montaner in 1905 and completed by his son in 1930, the Hospital de la Santa Creu de Sant Pau's pavilions are lavishly embellished with mosaics, stained glass, and sculptures by Eusebi Arnau. The octagonal columns with floral capitals are inspired by those in the Monestir de Santes Creus (see p128), to the south of Barcelona.

1 Sagrada Família

Dizzying spires and intricate sculptures adorn Gaudí's magical masterpiece (see pp12–15). Construction began at the height of *Modernisme*, but is still in progress more than a century later.

2 La Pedrera

This amazing apartment block, with its curving façade and bizarre rooftop, has all of Gaudí's architectural trademarks (see pp26–7). Especially characteristic are the building's wrought-iron balconies and the ceramic mosaics decorating the entrance halls.

3 Sant Pau Recinte Modernista

In defiant contrast to the Eixample's symmetrical grid-like pattern, this ambitious

4 Fundació Tàpies

With a Rationalist, plain façade alleviated only by its Mudéjar-style brickwork, this building (see p108), dating from 1886, was home to the publishing house Montaner i Simón. It bears the distinction of being the first Modernista work to be designed by Domènech i Montaner, which explains why it has so few of the ornate decorative touches that distinguish his later works. Today it is home to the Fundació Tàpies, and is dominated by an enormous sculpture by the Catalan artist.

5 Casa Batlló

MAP E2 ■ Pg de Gràcia 43
■ Open 9am–8:15pm daily ■ Adm (audio guide) ■ www.casabatllo.es

Illustrating Gaudí's nationalist sentiments, Casa Batlló, on La

Hospital de la Santa Creu i de Sant Pau

olourful exterior of Casa Batlló

lansana de la Discòrdia *(see p107)*, a representation of the Sant Jordi ory *(see p41)*. The roof is the dragon's ack; the balconies, in the form of arnival masks, are the skulls of the ragon's victims. The façade exem-lifies Gaudí's remarkable use of blour and texture.

⑥ Casa Amatller
MAP E2 ▪ Pg de Gràcia 41
Open 10am–6pm daily; guided nd audio tours only ▪ Adm ▪ www. matller.org

he top of Casa Amatller's façade ursts into a brilliant display of blue, ream and pink tiles with burgundy orets. Architect Puig i Cadafalch's xaggerated decorative use of ceram-cs is typical of *Modernisme*. Tours nclude the Modernista apartment nd a slide show in Amatller's former hotography studio *(see p107)*, and escribe the neo-medieval vestibule.

⑦ Casa de les Punxes (Casa Terrades)
v Diagonal 420 ▪ Adm
www.casadelespunxes.com

aking *Modernisme*'s Gothic and nedieval obsessions to extremes hat others seldom dared, Puig i Cadafalch created this imposing, astle-like structure between 1903 nd 1905 *(see p108)*. Given the nick-ame Casa de les Punxes or "House f Spines" because of the sharp, eedle-like spires that rise up from s conical turrets, the building's eal name is Casa Terrades, for its riginal owners. The flamboyant

spires contrast with a façade that is sparsely decorated. The building is now used as a co-working space.

⑧ Palau de la Música Catalana
Domènech i Montaner's magnificent concert hall is a joyous celebration of Catalan music *(see pp32–3)*. Ablaze with mosaic friezes, stained glass, ceramics and sculptures, it displays Modernista style in its full glory. The work of Miquel Blay on the façade is rated as one of the best examples of Modernista sculpture in Barcelona.

⑨ Casa Vicens
A UNESCO World Heritage Site, Casa Vicens *(see p119)* was the first home designed by Antoni Gaudí. The façade is an explosion of colour, at once austere and flamboyant, with Neo-Mudéjar elements and sgraffito floral motifs. The building now func-tions as a cultural centre. Inside, you will find perfectly preserved residen-tial rooms with original furniture and paintings. Down in the coal cellar is a fascinating underground bookshop.

⑩ Palau Güell
The use of parabolic arches here *(see p87)* to orchestrate space is an example of Gaudí's experiments with structure. He also used unusual building materials, such as ebony and rare South American woods.

Arched interiors of Palau Güell

🔟 Public Squares

Stately Plaça Reial, surrounded by Neo-Classical buildings and palm trees

① Plaça Reial

The arcaded Plaça Reial *(see p78)*, in the heart of the Barri Gòtic, is unique among Barcelona's public squares due to its old-world charm, gritty urbanization and Neo-Classical flair. It is home not only to fascinating Gaudí lampposts and majestic mid-19th-century buildings, but also to a slew of buzzing bars and cafés, and an entertaining and colourful crowd of inner-city Barcelona denizens.

② Plaça de Catalunya
MAP M1

Barcelona's nerve centre is the huge Plaça de Catalunya, a lively hub from which the city's activity seems to radiate. This square is most visitors' first real glimpse of Barcelona. The airport bus stops here, as do RENFE trains and countless metro and bus lines, including most night buses. The square's commercial swagger is evident all around, headed by Spain's omnipresent department store, El Corte Inglés *(see p66)*. Pigeons flutter chaotically at the square's centre and travellers wander about. The main tourist information office is located here. Concerts are held in the square during festivals.

③ Plaça del Rei
MAP N4

One of the city's best-preserved medieval squares, the Barri Gòtic's Plaça del Rei is ringed by grand historic buildings. Among them is the 14th-century Palau Reial *(see p78)*, which houses the Saló del Tinell, a spacious Catalan Gothic throne room and banqueting hall.

④ Plaça de Sant Jaume

Laden with power and history, this is the administrative heart *(see p77)* of modern-day Barcelona. The *plaça* is flanked by the city's two key government buildings, the stately Palau de la Generalitat and the 15th-century Ajuntament.

Plaça de Catalunya

5 Plaça de la Vila de Gràcia
MAP F1

The progressive, bohemian area of Gràcia, a former village annexed by Barcelona in 1897, still exudes a small-town ambience where socializing with the neighbours means heading for the nearest *plaça*. Topping the list is this atmospheric square, with an impressive clock tower rising at its centre. Bustling outdoor cafés draw buskers and a sociable crowd.

6 Plaça de Sant Josep Oriol and Plaça del Pi
MAP M3 & M4

Old-world charm meets modern café culture in the Barri Gòtic's leafy Plaça de Sant Josep Oriol and Plaça del Pi, named after the pine trees (*pi* in Catalan) that shade its nooks and crannies. The lovely Gothic church of Santa Maria del Pi *(see p41)* is set between the two squares.

7 Plaça Comercial
MAP P4

The buzzing Passeig del Born culminates in Plaça Comercial, an inviting square dotted with cafés and bars. It faces the 19th-century Born Market *(see p78)*, which has been transformed into a cultural centre and exhibition space.

8 Plaça de Santa Maria
MAP N5

The magnificent Església de Santa Maria del Mar *(see p78)* imbues its namesake *plaça*, in the El Born district, featuring a certain spiritual

Cafés on Plaça de Santa Maria

calm. Bask in its Gothic ambience, people watch, and soak up the sun at one of the outdoor terrace cafés.

9 Plaça del Sol
MAP F1

Tucked within the cosy grid of Gràcia, this square, popularly called Plaça del Encants, is surrounded by handsome 19th-century buildings. As evening descends, it transforms into one of the most lively spots for after-dark festivities, and you can join all the *Barcelonins* who come here to mingle on the outdoor terraces.

10 Plaça de la Vila de Madrid
MAP M2

Mere steps from the busy La Rambla *(see pp16–17)* is this spacious *plaça*, graced with the remains of a Roman necropolis. A remnant of Roman Barcino, the square sat just beyond the boundaries of the walled Roman city. A row of unadorned 2nd to 4th-century tombs was discovered here in 1957. The complete remains can be viewed from street level.

🔟 Parks and Beaches

1 Parc de Cervantes
Av Diagonal 708 ▪ Open 10am–dusk daily

Built in 1964 to celebrate 25 years of Franco's rule, this beautiful park on the outskirts of Barcelona would have been more appropriately named Park of the Roses. There are over 11,000 rose bushes of 245 varieties; when in bloom, their scent pervades the entire park. People pour in at weekends, but the park is blissfully deserted during the week.

2 Park Güell
The twisting pathways and avenues of columned arches of Park Güell (see pp22–3) blend in with the lush hillside, playfully fusing nature and fantasy to create an urban paradise. From the esplanade, with its stunning mosaic bench, visitors have spectacular views of the city and of the fairy-tale gatehouses below.

3 Jardins del Palau de Pedralbes
Av Diagonal 686 ▪ Open 10am–dusk daily

These picturesque, perfectly manicured gardens lie right in front of the former Palau Reial (royal palace) of Pedralbes. Under an enormous eucalyptus tree, near a small bamboo forest, stands the Fountain of Hercules designed by Gaudí. Discovered only in 1984, the fountain features a wrought-iron dragon-head spout.

Cascada fountain, Parc de la Ciutadella

4 Parc de la Ciutadella
The largest landscaped park in Barcelona (see p101) offers a refreshingly green, tranquil antidote to city life. Once the location of the 18th-century military citadel, this lovely, serene 19th-century park is now home to the city zoo, the Catalan parliament, a placid boating lake and a variety of works by Catalan sculptors as well as modern artists. It also has the extravagant Cascada Monumental, a two-tiered fountain, which Gaudí helped design.

Vibrant mosaic at Park Güell

5 Parc del Laberint d'Horta
Dating back to 1791, these enchanting gardens are among the city's oldest. Situated above the city, where the air is cooler and cleaner, the park includes themed

Parc del Laberint d'Horta

gardens, waterfalls and a small canal (see p118). The highlight is the vast maze with a statue of Eros at its centre. There is a picnic area and a children's playground at the entrance to the gardens.

6 Parc de Joan Miró
MAP B2 ■ C/Tarragona 74
■ Open 10am–dusk daily

Also known as Parc de l'Escorxador, this park in Eixample was built on the site of a 19th-century slaughter-house (escorxador). Dominating the paved upper level of the park is Miró's striking 22-m (72-ft) sculpture, Dona i Ocell (Woman and Bird), created in 1983. There are several play areas for kids and a couple of kiosk cafés.

7 Parc de l'Espanya Industrial
C/Muntadas 37 ■ Open 10am–midnight daily

Located on the site of a former textile factory, this modern park was built in 1986 by Basque architect Luis Peña Ganchegui. It is an appealing recrea-tional space, with 10 lighthouse-style viewing towers lined along one side of the lake and an enormous cast-iron dragon that doubles as a slide. There is a good terrace bar with a playground for kids.

8 City Beaches
The beaches of Barcelona were once insalubrious areas to be avoided. With the 1992 Olympics they underwent a radical face-lift. Today, the stretches of the Port Olímpic and Barceloneta are a people magnet (see p101). A short hop on the metro from the city centre, the beaches are regularly cleaned and the facilities include showers, toilets, play areas for kids, volleyball nets and an open-air gym. Boats and surfboards can be hired. Be aware, though, that bag snatching is endemic in these areas.

Enjoying watersports at Castelldefels

9 Castelldefels
Train to Platja de Castelldefels from Estació de Sants or Passeig de Gràcia

Just 20 km (12 miles) south of the city are 5 km (3 miles) of wide sandy beaches with shallow waters, ideal for watersports. Beach bars entice weekend sun worshippers out of the afternoon sun for long, lazy seafood lunches and jugs of sangria. Wind-surfers are available for hire.

10 Premià de Mar and El Masnou
Train to Premià or El Masnou from Plaça de Catalunya or Estació de Sants

Arguably the best set of beaches within easy reach of Barcelona, just 20 km (12 miles) to the north of the city, these two adjoining beaches lure locals and visitors alike with golden sand and clear, blue waters.

🔟 Off the Beaten Track

Dragon, Güell Pavilions gate

1 Güell Pavilions
MAP B2 ■ Av Pedralbes 7
■ 93 317 76 52 ■ Open 10am–4pm
daily; call ahead for guided visits (93
256 25 04) ■ Adm

Gaudí designed the gatehouses
and stable, known collectively as
the Güell Pavilions *(see p78)*,
for his patron Eusebi Güell
in the 1880s. You can admire
the enormous dragon,
inspired by the myth of the
Garden of the Hesperides,
which lunges out of the
wrought-iron gate, and
visit the complex as part
of a guided tour.

2 Jardins de la Rambla de Sants
MAP A2 ■ C/d'Antoni de Capmany s/n

This elevated park, which stretches
for almost a kilometre from the
Plaça de Sants to the La Bordeta
district, is built above a disused
railway track. It provides a peaceful
stroll, with some refreshing bursts
of greenery, in amongst the high-
rise apartment blocks and old
factory buildings.

3 El Refugi 307
MAP C5 ■ C/Nou de la Rambla
175 ■ 93 256 21 22 ■ Guided tours
at 10:30am in English on Sun, and
by appointment ■ Adm ■ www.
barcelona.cat/museuhistoria/
en/heritages

More than a thousand underground
shelters were built beneath the city
during the Spanish Civil War, when
Barcelona was being bombed by the
nationalist forces. Shelter 307, with
400 m (1,312 ft) of tunnels, contained
an infirmary, a toilet, a water fountain
a fireplace and a children's room. It
is now part of the Museu d'Història
de Barcelona *(see p78)* and provides
a glimpse into the torment endured
by city residents during the war.

4 Mercat de la Llibertat
Pl Llibertat 27 ■ 93 413 23 23
■ Open 8:30am–8:30pm Mon–Fri (to
3pm Sat); timings of stalls may vary

The Mercat de la Llibertat in Gràcia
was built in 1888 and is notable
for its beautiful wrought-iron and
ceramic decoration. As well as a
fabulous range of fresh produce,
it also has excellent stalls selling everything from original
photographs to fashions.

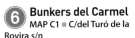

Pavilion, Parc del Laberint d'Horta

5 Parc del Laberint d'Horta
These lovely 18th-century
gardens *(see p118)* are filled
with classical statuary,
little pavilions and orna-
mental ponds, but it is
the fabulous and sur-
prisingly tricky maze at
their heart that is the big draw.

6 Bunkers del Carmel
MAP C1 ■ C/del Turó de la
Rovira s/n

Barcelona has a handful of disused
bunkers – a reminder of the aerial
attacks that took place during the
long Spanish civil war. Chiselled into
the side of a hill in the working-class
El Carmel district, the roof of this

bunker acts as a viewing platform. It's become a popular place to enjoy a few beers and contemplate the city's skyline as the sun goes down.

7 Basílica de la Puríssima Concepció

MAP F2 ■ C/d'Aragó 299 ■ Open 7:30am–1pm & 5–9pm Mon–Fri (Aug: to 8pm); 7:30am–2pm & 5–9pm Sun ■ www.parroquiaconcepciobcn.org

Dating back to the 13th century, this basilica was originally part of the Santa Maria de Jonqueres monastery. It was moved stone by stone to its current site in the 19th century. Head for the charming Gothic cloister, which is filled with greenery and birdsong, and bordered by slender 15th-century columns. The basilica regularly hosts concerts.

8 Convent de Sant Agustí

MAP F4 ■ Pl l'Academia /n, C/Comerç 36 ■ 93 256 50 17 ■ Open 9am–10pm Mon–Fri, 10am–2pm & 4–9pm Sat ■ Café: lunchtime Tue–Sat

The 15th-century Convent de Sant Agustí is now a cultural centre, with a lovely little café underneath the arches of what remains of the cloister. Relaxed and family-friendly, it is a great place to spend an afternoon.

9 Plaça Osca

MAP B2

This lovely, leafy old square in the Sants neighbourhood is flanked by cafés and bars, with tables spilling out onto the pavements. Rarely frequented by tourists but increasingly popular with trendy locals, the square has a clutch of great spots to enjoy artisan beer and some organic tapas.

10 Parc de Cervantes

Every spring, hundreds of people converge on the gardens in the Parc de Cervantes *(see p48)* to admire the blooms of 11,000 rose bushes of 245 varieties. Grassy lawns extend around the rose gardens, dotted with picnic areas and children's playgrounds.

The lush lawns and rose bushes of the Parc de Cervantes

🔟 Children's Attractions

Enjoying a thrilling ride at the Parc d'Atraccions del Tibidabo

1 Parc d'Atraccions del Tibidabo

With its old-fashioned rides, the only surviving funfair in the city is a delight *(see p117)*. The attractions include a roller coaster, a House of Horrors, bumper cars, a Ferris wheel and the Museu dels Autòmates *(see p43)*, with animatronics of all shapes and sizes. There's also a puppet show, picnic areas, playgrounds and plenty of cafés and restaurants.

2 La Rambla

Your shoulders will be aching from carrying the kids high above the crowds by the time you reach the end of Barcelona's main boulevard *(see pp16–17)*. Fire eaters, buskers, human statues dressed up as Greek goddesses – you name it and it's likely to be keeping the hordes entertained on La Rambla.

3 Museu Marítim

Ancient maps showing monster-filled seas, restored fishing boats and a collection of ships' figureheads give a taste of the city's maritime history *(see p87)*. Well worth a look is the full-size Spanish galleon complete with sound and light effects. Set in the vast former medieval shipyards, the Drassanes, this museum is an absolute must for any budding sea captain.

4 Parc de l'Oreneta

MAP A1 ■ Tren de l'Oreneta: www.trenoreneta.com

This delightful, shaded park has paths winding up the hillside, lots of play parks and picnic areas, as well as a paddock where kids can take pony rides. Perhaps the best of all is the miniature train (Tren de l'Oreneta), which makes a 650-m (2,130-ft) lap around the park from a tiny station.

Parc del Laberint d'Horta maze

5 Parc del Laberint d'Horta

The main feature of this exceptionally beautiful park *(see p118)* is the huge hedge maze where children can live out all of their *Alice in Wonderland* fantasies. Unfulfilled expectations of Mad Hatters are made up for by a play area and a bar for grown-ups. The park is usually busy on Sundays.

6 Telefèric de Montjuïc

MAP C5 ■ Parc de Montjuïc ■ Open Jan–Feb & Nov–Dec: 10am–6pm daily (Mar–May & Oct: to 7pm; Jun–Sep: to 9pm) ■ Adm ■ www.teleferic demontjuic.cat

Instead of taking the nerve-jangling cable-car ride across the port, try these smaller, lower-altitude cable-car trips if you have children with you. The ride to the Montjuïc summit also has the added appeal of the castle *(see p95)* at the top, with cannons for the kids to clamber on.

7 FC Barcelona Museum and Stadium Tour

Football fans can follow in the footsteps of their favourite players at the FC Barcelona Museum and Stadium Tour. See the changing rooms where the player prepare, explore the legendary stadium and get hands-on with interactive displays *(see p118)*. Barça's impressive array of trophies are another big draw.

8 City Beaches

For kids, there's more to going to the beach in Barcelona than just splashing in warm waters and frolicking in the sand. The Port Vell and Port Olímpic *platges* (beaches) offer a good choice of well-equipped play areas to keep the little ones entertained *(see p101)*. Numerous bars and restaurants make finding refreshment easy too.

9 Museu d'Història de Catalunya

This museum traces Catalonia's history through a range of inter-active exhibits *(see p101)*. Visitors can dress up as medieval knights and gallop around on wooden horses. Very popular with Catalan school groups, the museum is enjoyable for visitors of all ages. In addition toits stock of children's activities, it hosts an exciting story hour every Saturday wherein Catalan legends are re-enacted.

10 Boat Trips

The city's charming "swallow boats", Las Golondrinas *(see p102)*, make regular sight-seeing trips out of the port, providing a fun excursion for older children. Younger kids will probably prefer messing about in a rowing boat on the lake at the Parc de la Ciutadella *(see p48)*.

Boating on the Ciutadella lake

🔟 Performing Arts and Music Venues

Palau de la Música Catalana

1 Palau de la Música Catalana
Domenèch i Montaner's Modernista gem regularly serves up the best in jazz and classical music *(see pp32–3)*. It has lost some of its prestige to L'Auditori, but it still hosts some performances for Barcelona's Guitar Festival and also attracts visiting musicians.

2 Palau Sant Jordi and Sant Jordi Club
MAP A4 ■ Passeig Olímpic 5-7 ■ www.palausantjordi.barcelona
Once the stadium that formed the centrepiece of the1992 Olympics, the Palau Sant Jordi now stages some of the biggest acts to visit Barcelona. The adjoining Sant Jordi Club also hosts concerts.

3 Teatre Grec
This open-air amphitheatre, situated amid thick, verdant forest, makes an incredible setting for ballet, music or theatre *(see p96)*. Originally a quarry, it was converted in 1929 in preparation for the International Exhibition. It is open daily except during the summertime El Grec arts festival.

4 L'Auditori
MAP G1 ■ C/Lepant 150 ■ 93 247 93 00 ■ www.auditori.cat
Located near the Teatre Nacional, this large auditorium is home to the Orquestra Simfònica de Barcelona and also houses the Museum of Music. Acoustics and visibility are excellent. In addition to classical music, it hosts regular jazz concerts.

5 Gran Teatre del Liceu
Phoenix-like, the Liceu *(see p16)* has risen from the ashes of two devastating fires since its founding in 1847 to become one of Europe's leading opera houses. Originally designed to house the Music Conservatory, it now also hosts ballet productions and symphony concerts. It is known for sterling performances by home-grown talent including one of the famed "three tenors", José Carreras.

6 Harlem Jazz Club
The legendary Harlem Jazz Club *(see p83)* in Barrí Gòtic is one of the city's longest surviving jazz and blues clubs. As well as presenting great artistes, the admission charge usually includes a drink, and some shows are free.

Saxophonist at the Harlem Jazz Club

7 Mercat de les Flors
MAP B4 ■ C/Lleida 59 ■ 93 256 26 00 ■ www.mercatflors.cat
The venue of choice for dance and performance theatre groups such as

La Fura dels Baus and Comediants, whose incredible mixture of circus and drama is easily accessible to non-Catalan speakers.

8 **Razzmatazz**
This is one of the city's most famous venues (see p104). Hosting concerts several nights a week, the club's five areas offer a wide range of musical styles.

Vampire Weekend at Razzmatazz

9 **Sala Apolo**
MAP K4 ▪ C/Nou de la Rambla 113 ▪ 93 441 40 01 ▪ www.sala-apolo.com
A vintage dance hall with panelled bars and velvet-covered balconies, this place has reinvented itself as one of Barcelona's biggest and best nightclubs. It attracts the latest acts in music, from indie, garage and pop rock (Mondays), to reggae, soul, world music and dubstep (Thursdays).

10 **Milano Jazz Club**
With its red velvet banquettes and low lighting, this atmospheric cocktail bar and supper club (see p111) also doubles as an elegant jazz venue, with live music from Thursday to Sunday. Note that there are usually two live music sessions: one at 7:30pm and the other at 9:30pm. Doors open at 7pm.

TOP 10 VERSIÓN ORIGINAL CINEMAS AND FESTIVALS

Interior of the Filmoteca cinema

1 Filmoteca
www.filmoteca.cat
The Catalan government's film and media archive and cinema.

2 Verdi
MAP B2 ▪ C/Verdi 32 ▪ 93 238 79 90 ▪ www.cines-verdi.com
An original VO cinema with five screens.

3 Icària Yelmo Cineplex
MAP H5 ▪ C/Salvador Espriu 61 ▪ 90 222 09 22 ▪ www.yelmocines.es
With 15 screens, this cineplex shows VO films, many of them for children.

4 Festival de Cine Documental Musical In-Edit
www.in-edit.org
This international festival celebrates music and film.

5 Festival Internacional de Cinema Fantàstic de Catalunya
Sitges ▪ https://sitgesfilmfestival.com
A festival dedicated to VO fantasy films.

6 Zumzeig Cine Cooperativa
C/Béjar 53 ▪ www.zumzeigcine.coop
This cinema screens independent films.

7 Cinemes Texas
MAP F1 ▪ C/Bailen 205 ▪ 93 348 47 70 ▪ www.cinemestexas.cat
A modern cinema that shows VO films.

8 Sala Phenomena Experience
MAP G1 ▪ C/Sant Antoni Maria Claret 168 ▪ www.phenomena-experience.com
State-of-the-art cinema, one of the largest in Spain, for VO films.

9 Renoir Floridablanca
MAP C3 ▪ C/Floridablanca 135 ▪ 93 228 93 93 ▪ www.cinesrenoir.com
Vintage projectors are on display at this theatre screening international films.

10 Sala Montjuïc
MAP B6 ▪ www.salamontjuic.org
This outdoor cinema near the castle shows cult films in summer.

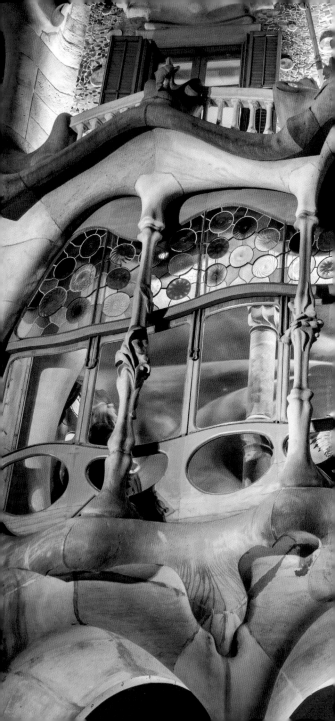

🔝 Photo Spots

1 Font Màgica

You can take some extraordinary photos of Barcelona's enchanting and exuberant "Magic Fountain" (see p70), which is linked by a long, choreographed line of smaller fountains, all the way up to the Palau Nacional (see p95). Set your shutter speed for a long exposure to get fluid, draping shots of the cascading water. At night, the fountain lights up with brilliant colour.

2 Rooftop of the Barcelona Cathedral

For a bird's-eye view of the impressive narrow lanes and alleys of Barri Gòtic (see pp76–79), climb up to the roof terrace of the Barcelona Cathedral (see pp18–19), where gargoyles and the carved stone of the central spire vie for attention.

3 Park Güell

Gaudí's fairy-tale imagination was let loose on this spectacular park (see pp22–3). The colourfully tiled salamander at the entrance staircase and the stunning panorama from the sinuous bench on the main square are the classic postcard views. There are scores of other exquisite details that will catch every photographer's eye.

Plaça de Sant Felip Neri at dusk

4 Plaça de Sant Felip Neri

The labyrinthine alleys and squares that make up Barri Gòtic (see pp76–79) are a photographer's dream. The little Plaça de Sant Felip Neri (see p80), with its charming church and simple stone fountain, provides a beautiful set piece for a photo. It also features numerous historical elements that make it attractive.

5 Museu d'Història de Catalunya

The café on the top floor of the Museu d'Història de Catalunya (see p101) offers dazzling views over the yacht-filled Port Vell (see p92) and up to the slopes of Montjuïc (see p125). It is a good idea to come at dusk to capture some of the best photos of Barcelona.

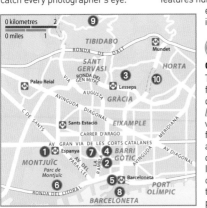

6 Castell de Montjuïc

This castle's bastions *(see p95)* enjoy one of the best vantage points over the entire city and offer incredible, panoramic views, which enable you to place several landmarks in the same frame. For a photo of a different side to the city, take some shots of the multicoloured shipping containers in the port.

7 Museu d'Art Contemporani

Barcelona's contemporary art museum, MACBA *(see pp34–5)*, is a striking white building overlooking a huge, modern square which has become a mecca for skateboarders. Their swift moves make for great action shots.

8 Beaches

It's hard to get a bad picture of the beaches *(see p101)*, in Barcelona whether you are visiting in the heat of summer or the relative calm of winter. A dawn shot of the tall, diaphanous sculpture, *The Wounded Star*, by Rebecca Horn on Barceloneta Beach is always a winner.

9 Tibidabo Ferris Wheel

Catch a ride on the charming and historic Ferris wheel at the Tibidabo funfair

The colourful Ferris wheel at Tibidabo

(see p117) to recreate a classic Barcelona shot: the pretty, rainbow-coloured cars juxtaposed against the sights of the entire city laid out at your feet.

10 Bunkers del Carmel
MAP E6

There are wonderful panoramic views to be had from these bunkers *(see pp50–51)* that date back to the Spanish Civil War. Tucked away in a quiet suburb, this is the perfect spot for a view of the city lights as the sun sets. In fact, these are now one of the city's most photographed viewpoints.

Visitors admiring the city from Bunkers del Carmel

🔟 Outdoor Bars

Diners outside Bar Kasparo

1 Bar Kasparo

This laid-back outdoor bar *(see p92)* serves a varied menu of fresh international fare made with a modern twist. Must-try dishes here include chicken curry and Greek salad. With outdoor seating in a quiet, traffic-free square, this bar is great for whiling away time. By day this is a popular spot with families, thanks to the play area it overlooks, but after the sun dips beneath the horizon a bar-like vibe takes over, fuelled by beer and cider.

2 Antic Teatre Café-Bar

Tucked away in a minuscule alley, this leafy outdoor bar *(see p83)* is attached to a theatre and is a popular meeting place for actors and musicians. Perfect for a quiet coffee during the day, the bar has a relaxed atmosphere. Once night falls, it is transformed into a magical secret garden. Sit on the terrace or in the garden, and enjoy a glass of wine.

3 El Jardí

The Gothic courtyard of a medieval hospital *(see p89)* provides a beautiful backdrop to this outdoor café, which is a quiet oasis in the heart of El Raval. The tables are arranged around a pretty garden, strung with fairy lights. It's a great spot for winding down with a cocktail after a day of sightseeing.

4 La Caseta del Migdia

Situated in the pine forest behind Montjuic Castle, this is a summer-only bar *(see p99)*. Fabulous views, ice-cold beers and the occasional live jazz concert or DJ session make this an irresistable spot to escape the heat on sultry summer nights and watch the sunset.

The terrace of La Caseta del Migdia

5 Bar Calders

Carrer del Parlament is packed with trendy boutiques and restaurants, but Bar Calders (see p99) stands out for its charming terrace, tasty tapas and delightful staff. It's one of the best places in the city for a *vermut* (see p65) and a dish of olives.

6 Torre Rosa

Located in the courtyard of a pink-hued centenary villa, this bar (see p122) provides the perfect summer retreat, away from the hustle and bustle of the city. Come here to enjoy expertly mixed cocktails under the cool shade of palm trees – as the locals do.

7 Cotton Hotel Terrace

Housed in a listed landmark building, now a luxury hotel, this enormous terrace bar (see p111) is furnished with plush chairs and sofas that are shaded by numerous luxuriant plants. It's a fashionable address to enjoy wines, excellent cocktails and upmarket tapas.

8 Jardín del Alma

It's hard to believe that you are in the middle of a metropolitan city once you step into this beautiful and deeply romantic garden retreat. Jardín del Alma (see p111) forms part of the elegant Alma Barcelona Hotel (see p142). Come here for fine wines, cocktails, as well as quite a few exquisite tapas, and stay for the ambience.

9 Fragments Cafè

A friendly local café located in one of the loveliest squares in the city, Fragments Café (see p123) is not the place to eat in a hurry. Take your time and and enjoy your meal in the pretty, plant-filled

garden at the back, where you can dine by candle light on balmy summer evenings.

10 Bus Terraza

A London double decker bus pulled up by the seafront has become one of Barcelona's hottest spots. There are always queues to get into this colourful garden terrace (see p104). Sink into one of the comfortable deckchairs or loungers, and enjoy DJ sets and live music with your cocktail.

DJ booth at Bus Terraza

🔟 Restaurants and Tapas Bars

The plush interior of La Taverna del Clínic

1 La Taverna del Clínic

Slightly off the beaten track, this upmarket tavern *(see p113)* offers inventive, though pricey tapas, accompanied by a great array of wines. The restaurant is popular with Barcelonans so arrive early or be prepared to wait for a table.

2 Igueldo

Basque cuisine, prepared with flair and originality, is served here in elegant surroundings *(see p113)*. Dishes include pig's trotters stuffed with *morcilla* (black pudding) and dried peach purée, or *zamburiñas*, a small scallop from the Atlantic.

3 El Asador d'Aranda

This palatial restaurant *(see p123)*, perched high above the city on Tibidabo, is popular with businesspeople and dishes up the best in Castilian cuisine. Sizable starters include *pica pica*, a tasty array of sausages, peppers and hams. The restaurant's signature main dish is *lechazo* (young lamb), roasted in a wood-fired oven.

4 Green Spot

Voted one of the best vegetarian restaurants in Spain, Green Spot *(see p105)* will also appeal to non-vegetarians. The contemporary cuisine, served in a spacious and stylish setting, is based on locally sourced, mainly organic produce. The dishes incorporate flavours from around the world.

5 Windsor

The modern Catalan *haute cuisine* dishes served in this elegant restaurant *(see p113)* are based on seasonal local produce. Tasting menus feature *suquet de rape* (monkfish stew) and suckling lamb.

The bar area at Windsor

6 Alkimia
MAP D3 ∎ Ronda de San Antoni 41 ∎ 93 207 61 15 ∎ Closed Sat–Mon ∎ €€

Jordi Vilà has won countless awards and a Michelin star for his innovative New Catalan cuisine, taking time-honoured dishes and giving them an artful twist. This restaurant inside the Cervecería Moritz offers a suitably spectacular setting.

7 Cinc Sentits
This elegant Michelin-starred restaurant (see p113) is known for its inventive cuisine. The tasting menu by chef Jordi Artal can be paired with specially chosen wines.

8 Pez Vela
Pg del Mare Nostrum 19/21 ∎ 93 221 63 17 ∎ €€

Contemporary decor and fresh Mediterranean cuisine coupled with some of the best sea views in the city make this a great spot for a special meal. Pez Vela is located underneath the W Barcelona hotel (see p143).

9 Enigma
C/Sepulveda 38 ∎ 616 696 322 ∎ Closed Mon–Fri L, Sat & Sun ∎ €€€

Legendary Barcelonan chef Albert Adrià heads several restaurants in the city, including Enigma. Styled as a gastronomic experience, it offers tapas-style sharing plates plus a constantly changing menu based on whatever is in season. The fantastical space, which has an atmospheric ceiling of clouds, provides a drama-tic backdrop for Adrià's creations.

10 Disfrutar
Avant-garde cuisine prepared by former El Bulli chefs is served here. The restaurant (see p113) has a well-lit, whitewashed interior that was designed as a homage to the fishing villages of Costa Brava. It also has a charming terrace. Enjoy unconventional dishes such as a gazpacho sandwich (sourdough with feta spread and raw vegetables) or Moroccan-style pigeon in their relaxed and modern setting.

TOP 10 TAPAS DISHES

Calamars a la Romana

1 Calamars
A savoury seafood option is *calamars a la romana* (deep-fried battered squid) or *calamars a la planxa* (grilled squid).

2 Patates Braves
This traditional tapas favourite consists of fried potatoes topped with a spicy sauce. Equally tasty are *patates* heaped with aioli (garlic and olive oil sauce).

3 Pa amb Tomàquet
A key part of any traditional tapas spread is this bread topped with tomato and olive oil.

4 Croquetes
These tasty fried morsels, usually prepared with cod, ham or chicken in a béchamel sauce, are all-time favourites.

5 Musclos o Escopinyes
Sample Barcelona's fruits of the sea with tapas of tasty mussels or cockles.

6 Truita de Patates
The most common tapas dish is this thick potato omelette, often topped with aioli (*allioli* in Catalan).

7 Ensaladilla Russa
"Russian salad" includes potatoes, onions, tuna (and often peas, carrots and other vegetables) all generously enveloped in mayonnaise.

8 Gambes a l'Allet
An appetizing dish of prawns fried in garlic and olive oil.

9 Pernil Serrà
Cured ham is a Spanish obsession. The best, and most expensive, is Extremadura's speciality, Jabugo.

10 Fuet
Embotits (Catalan sausages) include the ever-popular *fuet*, a dry, flavourful variety most famously produced in the Catalonian town of Vic.

For a key to restaurant price ranges see p85

🔟 Cafés and Light Bites

① Bistrot Levante
MAP M3 ▪ Placeta de Manuel Ribe ▪ 93 858 26 79 ▪ www.bistrot levante.com

Hidden in one of the alleys of the old city, this café offers breakfast, brunch and light dishes inspired by eastern Mediterranean cuisine. Sit out on the pretty square or in the cosy interior and tuck into homemade cakes, salads, hummus and baba ghanoush.

② Café de l'Òpera
MAP L4 ▪ La Rambla 74
▪ www.cafeoperabcn.com

Unwind in an elegant setting at this late 19th-century café while being tended to by vested *cambrers* (waiters). This former *xocolateria* (confectionery café) – named after the Liceu opera house opposite – serves fine gooey delights such as *xurros amb xocolata* (strips of fried dough with thick chocolate). It's the perfect little nook for people-watching on La Rambla.

Café de l'Òpera on La Rambla

The smart interior of Bar Lobo

③ Bar Lobo
MAP Q4 ▪ C/Pintor Fortuny 3
▪ 93 481 53 46

This chic café is a superb brunch spot during the day, but it really comes alive in the evenings. From Thursday to Saturday it opens until 1:30am for drinks. The terrace is very popular.

④ Laie Llibreria Cafè
Tuck into a generous buffet of rice, pasta, greens, chicken and more at this charming, long-running Eixample café-bookshop *(see p112)*. You can also opt for the well-priced vegetarian menu, which includes soup, salad and a main dish.

⑤ Federal Café
MAP D4 ▪ C/Parlament 39
▪ Closed Sun D ▪ www.federalcafe.es/barcelona

The airy Federal Café is a local hipster hang-out serving amazing coffee, brunch and light meals, as well as cocktails in the evening. There is also a romantic little roof terrace, free Wi-Fi and English-language magazines to flick through.

⑥ El Filferro
Bright and airy, this café *(see p105)* only has room for a few tables inside, with several more located out on the sunny square which is popular with families as it conveniently over-looks a playground. Fresh, creative Mediterranean dishes as well as tapas are served all day.

7 Alsur Café
MAP F3 ■ C/Roger de Llúria 23
■ 93 624 15 77 ■ www.alsurcafe.com

Its nonstop kitchen serves brunch, tapas, homemade cakes, sandwiches and salads. Free Wi-Fi, big windows and a warm atmosphere make it an ideal place to work or read the newspaper. There's also a branch in the El Born district and one in front of the Palau de la Música.

8 En Aparté
A light-filled café (see p84) serving a good selection of French cheeses and cold meats accompanied by French wines. The crème brûlée is a must and the fixed price lunch menu is good value. There are tables outside overlooking the square.

9 Granja Dulcinea
MAP L3 ■ C/Petritxol 2 ■ www.granjadulcinea.com

The xocolateries and granjes on Carrer Petritxol (see p80) have been satiating sugar cravings for decades. Among them is this old-fashioned café with to-die-for delights from xurros amb xocolata to strawberries and whipped cream. In summer, refreshing orxates and granissats are on the menu.

Pastries at Granja Dulcinea

10 La Tartela
MAP B3 ■ C/Llanca 32
■ Closed Sun D & Mon

A pretty little spot near Plaça Espanya serving cakes, quiches, lasagna and outstanding coffee. It has a few pavement tables and great service.

TOP 10 CAFÉ DRINKS

A cup of strong *cigaló*

1 Cigaló
For coffee with a bite, try a *cigaló* (carajillo), which has a shot of either *conyac* (cognac), whisky or *ron* (rum).

2 Tallat and Café Sol
A *tallat* is a small cup of coffee with a dash of milk. A *cafè sol* is just plain coffee. In the summer, opt for either one *amb gel* (with ice).

3 Cafè amb llet
Traditionally enjoyed in the morning, *cafè amb llet* is a large milky coffee.

4 Orxata
This sweet, milky-white drink made from the tiger nut is a local summertime favourite.

5 Granissat
Slake your thirst with a cool *granissat*, a crushed-ice drink that is usually lemon-flavoured.

6 Aigua
Stay hydrated with *aigua mineral* (mineral water) – *amb gas* is sparkling, *sense gas*, still.

7 Cacaolat
A chocolate-milk concoction, which is one of Spain's most popular sweet drink exports.

8 Una Canya and Una Clara
Una canya is roughly a quarter litre of *cervesa de barril* (draught beer). *Una clara* is the same size but made up of equal parts beer and fizzy lemonade.

9 Cava
Catalonia's answer to champagne is its home-grown *cava* – Freixenet and Codorníu are the most famous brands.

10 Vermut
Fortified wine served with a spritz of soda water. Going out for the *vermutada* is a popular ritual for the locals.

TOP10 Shopping Destinations

2 Carrer Girona
MAP P1

Those looking for fashion bargains should head to Carrer Girona (metro Tetuan), which is lined with designer and high-street outlet stores. Most of these offer women's fashions including streetwear from brands such as Mango, evening wear and shoes from Catalan designers Etxart & Panno, and upmarket designs from the likes of Javier Simorra.

3 Plaça de Catalunya and Carrer Pelai
MAP L/M1 ■ El Corte Inglés: Pl de Catalunya 14; open 9:30am–9:30pm Mon–Sat ■ El Triangle: C/Pelai 39; open 9:30am–9pm Mon–Sat (Jun–Sep: to 10pm)

The city's bustling centrepiece is also its commercial crossroads, flanked by the department store El Corte Inglés and the shopping mall El Triangle, which includes FNAC (books, CDs, videos) and Séphora (perfumes and cosmetics). Lined with shops, the nearby Carrer Pelai is said to have more pedestrian traffic than any other shopping street in Spain.

1 Passeig de Gràcia
MAP E3

Set right in the heart of the city, Barcelona's grand avenue of lavish Modernista buildings is fittingly home to some of the city's premier fashion and design stores. From the international big league (Chanel, Gucci, Dior, Stella McCartney) to Spain's heavy hitters (Camper, Loewe, Zara, Bimba y Lola, Mango), it's all here. The wide boulevards either side feature more designer shopping, notably Carrer Consell de Cent, which is also dotted with many art galleries, and Carrers Mallorca, València and Roselló.

4 Maremagnum
MAP N5 ■ Muelle de España 5 ■ Open 10am–9pm daily

This shopping and entertainment centre is located right on the water's edge, and is open every day of the

Top design and fashion stores on Passeig de Gràcia

Visitors at the Maremagnum centre

year. All of the main clothing chains can be found here, along with a good variety of cafés and restaurants.

5 Portal de l'Àngel
MAP M2

Once a Roman thoroughfare leading into the walled city of Barcino, today the pedestrian street of Portal de l'Àngel is traversed by hordes of shoppers toting bulging bags. The street is chock-full of shoe, clothing, jewellery and accessory shops.

6 Rambla de Catalunya
MAP E2

The genteel, classier extension of La Rambla, this well-maintained street (see p109) offers a refreshing change from its cousin's more downmarket carnival atmosphere. Chic shops and cafés pepper the street's length from Plaça de Catalunya to Diagonal. Here you'll find everything from fine footwear and leather bags to linens and decorative lamps.

7 Carrer Portaferrissa
MAP M3

Offering an eclectic range of items, from zebra platform shoes to belly-button rings and pastel baby T-shirts, this street's other name could well be Carrer "Trendy". In addition to all the usual high-street chains – from H&M to Mango and NafNaf – along this strip you'll find El Mercadillo, crammed with hip little shops selling spiked belts, frameless sunglasses, surf wear and the like. After stocking

up on fashion, stop for a box of prettily wrapped chocolates at Fargas on the nearby Carrer del Pi (No. 16).

8 Gràcia
MAP F1

Old bookstores, family-run grocery stores and independent boutiques selling trendy, often vintage, fashion, homewares and accessories cluster along Carrer Astúries (and its side streets) and along Travessera de Gràcia. A string of contemporary clothing and shoe shops also line Gran de Gràcia.

9 El Born
MAP P4

Amid El Born's web of streets are all sorts of art and design shops (see p78). Passeig del Born and Carrer Rec are dotted with innovative little galleries (from sculpture to interior design), plus clothing and shoe boutiques. The best area for original fashion and accessories.

Handbag store, Avinguda Diagonal

10 Avinguda Diagonal
MAP D1

Big and brash, the traffic-choked Avinguda Diagonal is hard to miss – a cacophonous avenue that cuts diagonally across the entire city. It is a premier shopping street, particularly west of Passeig de Gràcia to its culmination in L'Illa mall and the huge El Corte Inglés department store close to Plaça Maria Cristina. Lining this long stretch is a host of high-end clothing and shoe stores – including Armani, Loewe and Hugo Boss – as well as a large number of interior design shops, jewellery and watch purveyors, and more.

Markets

1 Book and Coin Market at Mercat de Sant Antoni

MAP D2 ■ C/Comte d'Urgell ■ Open 8am–2:30pm Sun ■ www.mercat dominicaldesantantoni.com

For book lovers, there's no better way to spend Sunday morning than browsing at this market in Sant Antoni. You'll find a mind-boggling assortment of weathered paperbacks, ancient tomes, stacks of old magazines, comics, postcards and lots more, from coins to videos.

2 Fira de Santa Llúcia

MAP N3 ■ Pl de la Seu ■ Open 1–23 Dec: 10am–8pm (times may vary) daily

The festive season is officially under way when local artisans set up shop outside the cathedral for the annual Christmas fair. Well worth a visit, if only to peruse the *caganers*, miniature figures squatting to *fer caca* (take a poop). Uniquely Catalan, the *caganers* are usually hidden away at the back of nativity scenes. This unusual celebration of the scatological also appears in other Christmas traditions.

3 Els Encants

Trading beneath metal canopies, Els Encants *(see p108)* is one of Europe's oldest flea markets,

Stalls at Els Encants flea market

dating back to the 14th century. It sells everything from second-hand clothes, electrical appliances and toys to used books. Discerning shoppers can fit out an entire kitchen from the array of pots and pans available. Bargain-hunters should come early.

Produce at Mercat de la Boqueria

4 Mercat de la Boqueria

The most famous food market in Barcelona is conveniently located on La Rambla *(see pp16–17)*. Freshness reigns supreme and shoppers are spoiled for choice, with hundreds of stalls selling everything from vine-ripened tomatoes and haunches of beef to aromatic seafood and wedges of Manchego cheese. Be sure to stop by one of the atmospheric counter bars here. These are ideal for a quick lunch stop or a coffee break.

5 Fira Artesana

MAP M3 ■ Pl del Pi ■ Open 10am–10pm first & third Fri, Sat & Sun of the month

The Plaça del Pi *(see p47)* brims with natural and organic foods during the Fira Artesana, when artisanal food producers bring their goods to this corner of the Barri Gòtic. The market specializes in homemade cheeses and honey – from clear clover honey from the Pyrenees to nutty concoctions from Reus.

⑥ Fira de Filatelia i Numismàtica

MAP L4 ■ Pl Reial ■ Open 9am–2:30pm Sun

Arranged around the elegant Plaça Reial (see p78), this stamp and coin market draws avid collectors from across town. The newest collectors' items are phone cards and old xapes de cava (cava bottle cork foils). When the market ends – and the local police go to lunch – a makeshift flea market takes over. Old folks and immigrants from the barri haul out their antique wares – old lamps, clothing, junk – and lay it out for sale on the ground.

⑦ Mercat de Barceloneta

MAP F6 ■ Pl Font 1, Barceloneta ■ Open 7am–3pm Mon–Thu & Sat, 7am–8pm Fri ■ www.mercatsbcn.cat

The striking Barceloneta market overlooks an expansive square. In addition to colourful produce stalls, there is a good selection of bars and bakeries here.

⑧ Mercat dels Antiquaris

MAP N3 ■ Pl de la Seu ■ Open 10am–8pm Thu (except Aug) ■ www.mercatgoticbcn.com

Antiques aficionados and collectors contentedly rummage through vintage jewellery, watches, candelabras, embroidery and bric-a-brac at this long-running antiques market in front of the cathedral.

⑨ Mercat del Art de la Plaça de Sant Josep Oriol

MAP M4 ■ Pl de Sant Josep Oriol ■ Open 11am–8:30pm Sat, 10am–3pm Sun

At weekends, local artists flock to this Barri Gòtic square to set up their easels and sell their art. You'll find a range including watercolours of Catalan landscapes to oil paintings of churches and castles.

⑩ Mercat de Santa Caterina

MAP N3 ■ Av Francesc Cambó 16 ■ Open 7:30am–3:30pm Mon, Wed & Sat, 7:30am–8:30pm Tue, Thu & Fri ■ www.mercatsantacaterina.com

Each barri has its own food market with tempting displays but this one has a truly spectacular setting. The building was designed by Catalan architect Enric Miralles (1995–2000).

The striking Mercat de Santa Caterina

🔟 Barcelona for Free

Relaxing on a Barcelona beach

1 Beaches

Barcelona has 10 beaches, which collectively stretch for over 4.5 km (3 miles) along the coast. Between Easter and October they are dotted with *xiringuitos* selling drinks and snacks, and have lifeguards, sun lounger rental and even a beach library.

2 Sunday Afternoons at City Museums

www.barcelonaturisme.com/wv3/en/enjoy/25/a-zero-cost-cultural-afternoon.html

All city-run museums offer free admission at least one afternoon a month, usually the first Saturday or Sunday of the month, and several, including the Museu de Catalunya, Museu del Disseny, Centre de Cultura Contemporánea de Barcelona (CCCB), Museu de la Història de Barcelona (MUHBA) and Museu Blau (main site of the Museu de Ciències Naturals), are free Sunday afternoon from 3pm. A full list of these can be found on the Barcelona Turisme website.

3 Font Màgica

The Magic Fountain *(see p95)* thrills with its sound and light shows – in which multi-coloured jets of water leap to different soundtracks in elegant rows all the way up to the MNAC on the hill behind. The programme, ranging from classical to Disney tunes, is on the Barcelona Turisme website. Festes de la Mercè's closing event, the Piromusical (a fireworks and laser show), also takes place here.

4 Cinema Lliure al Platja

https://cinemalliure.com/platja

Platja beach hosts free screenings of independent films during the summer months. One evening a week (usually Thursdays) throughout July and August, locals settle down on beach towels at sunset to cool off on the sand while watching a movie. Sometimes there's live music beforehand, too. Check out the website for the summer schedule.

5 La Capella

MAP K3 ■ C/Hospital 56
■ Opening times vary, check website ■ https://lacapella.barcelona

The chapel at the Antic Hospital de la Santa Creu *(see p89)* has been converted into a fantastic art space hosting exhibitions of contemporary works by up-and-coming artists.

6 Festes

Every neighbourhood has its own *festa major* (various dates, Jun–Sep), ranging from the bacchanalian romp in Gràcia to the more modest celebrations of Poble Sec. You will see various Catalan traditions, from *castells* (human towers) to *correfocs* (fire-running) – and all for free. One of the biggest festivals is the Festes de la Mercè *(see p73)*.

Fireworks at the Festes de la Mercè

7 Spectacular Panoramas

With its wealth of *miradors* (viewpoints), Barcelona offers ample opportunity to contemplate the city's beauty. Relax over a glass of fizzing cava at Bunkers del Carmel *(see p50)* and enjoy views of the dazzling lights as the sun sets. Or head up to Mount Tibidabo, better known as 'the magic mountain', which is equally popular for the sublime vistas it offers.

8 Carretera de les Aigües

Running along the side of the Collserola park *(see p119)*, this path is popular with mountain-bikers and runners, and offers spectacular views across the city and out to sea. Getting there is fun too: take the FGC train to Peu de la Funicular, then ride the funicular up to the *carretera* stop.

The surrealist *Head of Barcelona*

9 Street Art

The streets are filled with art by world-renowned artists including Botero's *Cat* on the Rambla del Raval; Lichtenstein's *Head of Barcelona* and Mariscal's *Gambrinus* at the city port; Gehry's glittering *Fish* by the sea; and Miró's *Woman and Bird* in the Parc de Joan Miró *(see p49)* and mosaic at the Mercat de la Boqueria *(see p68)*.

10 Open House Barcelona

www.48hopenhouse barcelona.org

Peek into private homes and historic monuments during Barcelona's annual Open House weekend. Many buildings not usually open to the public can be explored, including the Arc de Triomf and the Ateneu cultural centre.

TOP 10 BUDGET TIPS

The Montjuïc parks

1 Pack a picnic of tasty local produce and head to the Montjuïc parks (the Parc Jacint Mossen Cinto with its lily ponds and shady nooks is a particular favourite) or to the beaches to dine for a fraction of the price of a restaurant.

2 If you are going to be visiting a lot of museums and using the public transport system, invest in the Barcelona Card, which starts at €48 for 72 hours.

3 The Art Ticket, which allows entry to six major art museums for €35 is an excellent deal for culture buffs.

4 Download the Too Good to Go app, which lists surplus food sold at reduced prices by restaurants and bakeries.

5 Several theatres and cinemas offer reduced prices on *Dia del Espectador*, usually Monday, Tuesday or Wednesday, or for the day's first performance (usually around 4pm).

6 At weekday lunchtimes, many restaurants serve a good-value *menú del migdia* with two or three courses, a glass of wine and perhaps a coffee.

7 The best travel option is the T-Casual, a travel card valid for 10 journeys in zones 1 to 6 and the airport train (not for the airport metro).

8 Some university residences, such as the Residència Àgora BCN and the Residència Erasmus, offer cheap beds during the summer break.

9 For fashion bargains, hit the outlet stores on Carrer Girona, near the Gran Via. Brands include Mango, Etxart & Panno and Nice Things.

10 All products offered by Barcelona's tourist service, from the Bus Turístic to walking tours, are sold at a discount (usually 10 per cent) on its website.

Festivals and Events

Performer at the Carnival in Sitges

1 Colourful Carnivals

Barcelona's week-long carnival season kicks off on Dijous Gras (last Thursday before Lent) with a parade up the Rambla. Led by the carnival king and queen, it culminates in a confetti battle. The buzzing beach town of Sitges *(see p127)* has the biggest celebration, with over-the-top floats carrying performers.

2 Llum BCN

In February, Barcelona's festival of light transforms the revitalized former warehouse district of Poblenou. The buildings, galleries and squares flicker with light sculptures, installations and shows in a stunning display.

3 El Dia de Sant Jordi

On 23 April, the day of Sant Jordi *(see p41)*, Barcelonans exchange books and roses, sold at open-air stalls across the city. The rose petals symbolize the blood of the slain dragon, while the books are a tribute to Cervantes and Shakespeare, who both died on 23 April 1616.

4 Summer Arrives

In celebration of St John and the start of summer, 23 June is Catalonians' night to play with fire – and play they do, with gusto. Fireworks streak through the night sky and bonfires are set ablaze on beaches and in towns throughout the region.

5 LGBTQ+ Events
www.pridebarcelona.org
■ www.circuitfestival.net/Barcelona

Barcelona has a lively LGBTQ+ scene, with specialist bookshops, hip boutiques and chic clubs that pulsate into the early hours. In June, the city celebrates Pride with fabulous floats, concerts and a full programme of talks and activities. The Circuit Festival in August is a sizzling event, where people flock to Barcelona's beaches for this huge LGBTQ+ party.

6 Castells

The tradition of building *castells* (human towers) in Catalonia dates back to the 18th century. In June, trained *castellers* stand on each others' shoulders to create a human castle – the highest tower takes the prize. *Castells* are often performed in Plaça Sant Jaume.

7 Neighbourhood Festivals

Barcelona is a city that enjoys a party. During the summer months every neighbourhood has some form of celebration. The best known *festa major* is in Gràcia in mid-August, famous for its extravagantly decorated streets and outdoor concerts. Other neighbourhood festivals include Poble Sec in July and Sants in August, both of which feature traditional parades and *correfocs* (fire-running).

Festa Major de Gràcia celebrations

Festes de la Mercè
www.barcelona.cat/lamerce

Barcelona's main festival is a riotous week-long celebration in honour of La Mercè, a co-patron saint of the city (*see p41*). The night sky lights up with fireworks, outdoor concerts are held, and there are parades of *gegants* and *capgrossos* (giants and fatheads). Don't miss the *correfoc* (fire-running), when fire-spitting dragons career through the streets.

Gegants, Festes de la Mercè

 The Big Screen
www.sitgesfilmfestival.com

Every October Barcelona hosts the glamorous Sitges Film Festival, the world's biggest celebration of fantasy and horror productions. Oudoor cinema is offered during the summer, with the *Gandules* (deckchairs) festival featuring arthouse films.

 Christmas Celebrations
The Nadal (Christmas) season begins on 1 December with festive artisan fairs. Fira de Santa Llúcia, Barcelona's oldest Christmas market, sees stalls set up around Catedral de Barcelona selling handmade gifts. On 5 January is the spectacular Cavalcada de Reis (Parade of the Three Kings). The kings arrive by ship into the city's harbour and then parade through streets lined with children. In Spain, the kings bring the children their presents on this magical night.

TOP 10 MUSIC, THEATRE AND ART FESTIVALS

Revellers at the Festival del Sónar

1 Guitar BCN
www.guitarbcn.com
International guitar festival organized by Spanish music promoters, The Project.

2 Jazz Terrassa
www.jazzterrassa.org
This internationally renowned festival offers jazz concerts in venues around the town of Terrassa.

3 Ciutat Flamenco
www.ciutatflamenco.com
A week of outstanding flamenco music and dance at venues around the city.

4 Primavera Sound
www.primaverasound.com
A pop, rock and underground dance music festival featuring many big names.

5 Festival del Sónar
www.sonar.es
This festival is an explosion of music and the latest in audiovisual production.

6 Grec Festival Barcelona
www.barcelona.cat/grec
Barcelona's largest music, theatre and dance festival.

7 Crüilla
www.cruillabarcelona.com
Huge summer festival in the Parc del Fòrum, with big name bands and emerging talent

8 Festival Jardins Pedralbes
www.festivalpedralbes.com
International names in rock and pop perform in the lovely Parc de Pedralbes.

9 Festival de Música Antiga
www.auditori.cat
A regular season of early music held at the prestigious venue L'Auditori.

10 Festival Internacional de Jazz de Barcelona
www.jazz.barcelona
Jazz festival with experimental music and big-names, held all over the city.

Barcelona
Area by Area

The stunning cityscape with the
Sagrada Família in the background

🔟 Barri Gòtic and La Riber

Starting as the Roman settlement of Barcino, the city grew over the years, culminating in a building boom in the 14th and 15th centuries. Barri Gòtic is a beautifully preserved neighbourhood of Gothic buildings, lively squares and atmospheric alleys. At its religious and social heart is the cathedral, a further reminder of the area's medieval heyday. Extending east of Barri Gòtic is the ancient *barri* of La Ribera, with lovely Carrer Montcada and the Museu Picasso.

Mosaic, Palau de la Música Catalana

BARRI GÒTIC AND LA RIBERA

1 Barcelona Cathedral
Soaring over the Barri Gòtic is Barcelona's mighty cathedral (see pp18–19), which dates from 1298.

2 Museu Picasso
Discover the youthful output (see pp30–31) of one of the most revered artists of the 20th century.

3 Palau de la Música Catalana
The city's most prestigious concert hall (see pp32–3) is a breathtaking monument to both *la música Catalana* and the Modernista aesthetic.

Façade of the Palau de la Generalitat

4 Plaça de Sant Jaume
MAP M4 ■ Palau de la Generalitat: 012; open 10:30am–1:30pm second & fourth Sat & Sun of the month for guided tours, reserve ahead; https://presidencia.gencat.cat/en/ambits_d_actuacio/palau-de-la-generalitat/visites-al-palau/index.html ■ Ajuntament: open 10am–1:30pm Sun for guided tours (English at 10am)

The site at which the Plaça de Sant Jaume (see p46) lies today was once the nucleus of Roman Barcino. With these roots, it seems fitting that the square is home to Barcelona's two most important government buildings – the Palau de la Generalitat (the seat of Catalonian parliament) and the Ajuntament (city hall). Look out for the detailed carved relief of Sant Jordi, Catalonia's patron saint, on the 15th-century Generalitat façade. Within is the beautiful 1434 Capella de Sant Jordi (see p41). A highlight of the Gothic 15th-century Ajuntament is the Saló de Cent, from where the Council of One Hundred, Barcelona's first form of government, ruled from 1372 to 1714. Also worth exploring is the Pati dels Tarongers, a lovely arcaded courtyard planted with orange trees and overlooked by interesting gargoyles.

EL BORN

If you're hankering for a proper martini or some alternative jazz, then look no further than El Born, a medieval neighbourhood that's been "reborn". Students and artists moved in, attracted by cheap rents and airy warehouses, fostering an arty vibe that now blends in with the area's old-time aura. Experimental design shops share the narrow streets with traditional balconied buildings festooned with laundry hung out to dry. Passeig de Born, lined with bars and cafés, leads onto the inviting Plaça Comercial, where the cavernous Born Market (in operation 1870–1970) has been converted into a cultural centre and exhibition space.

Three Graces fountain, Plaça Reial

its centre is a wrought-iron fountain representing the Three Graces. The palm-lined square has a cluster of restaurants, bars and cafés that are constantly busy.

5 Museu d'Història de Barcelona (MUHBA)

MAP M4 ■ Pl del Rei ■ Open 10am–2pm & 3–8pm Tue–Sun ■ Adm; free first Sun of the month, every Sun after 3pm ■ www.barcelona.cat/museuhistoria

The medieval Plaça del Rei (see p46) contains the core site of the Museu d'Història de Barcelona, encompassing remains ranging from Roman Barcino to the Middle Ages. These include Casa Padellàs (see p42) and the Palau Reial, which contains the Capella de Santa Àgata (see p41) and the Saló del Tinell, a massive arched hall where Ferdinand and Isabel met Columbus after his 1492 voyage to the Americas. The museum also has one of the largest underground excavations of Roman ruins on display in Europe (see p81), including a 3rd-century garum factory and winery.

6 Plaça Reial

MAP L4

Late 19th-century elegance meets sangria-drinking café society in the arcaded Plaça Reial, one of the city's most entertaining squares (see p46). The Modernista lampposts were designed by Gaudí in 1879, and at

7 Museu Frederic Marès

MAP N3 ■ Pl de Sant Iu 5–6 ■ Open 10am–7pm Tue–Sat, 11am–8pm Sun ■ Adm; free first Sun of the month, every Sun after 3pm ■ www.barcelona.cat/museufredericmares

This fascinating museum houses the collection of Catalan sculptor Frederic Marès. No mere hobby collector, the astute (and obsessive) Marès amassed holdings that a modern museum curator would die for. Among them are religious icons and statues, dating from Roman times to the present, and the curious "Museu Sentimental", which displays everything from ancient watches to fans and dolls. Also worth a visit during summer is Cafè d'Estiu (see p84), a sunny spot for a break on the museum's patio.

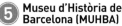

Museu Frederic Marès

8 Basilica de Santa Maria del Mar

MAP P5 ■ Pl de Santa Maria 1 ■ Open 10am–8:30pm daily; cultural visit: 10am–6pm Mon–Sat, 1:30–5:30pm Sun ■ Timings for guided tours vary, check website ■ Adm for guided tours, cultural visits and bell towers ■ https://santamariadelmarbarcelona.org

The spacious, breathtaking interior of this 14th-century church (see p40), designed by architect Berenguer de

Montagut, is a premier example of the austere Catalan Gothic style. The church is dedicated to St Mary of the Sea, the patron saint of sailors, and an ancient model ship hangs near one of the statues of the Virgin. Dubbed "the people's church", this is a popular spot for exchanging wedding vows. The rooftop, accessed via the bell towers, offers spectacular views.

⑨ Museu Etnològic i de Cultures del Món

MAP P4 ■ C/Montcada 14 ■ Open 10am–8:30pm daily ■ Adm; free first Sun of the month, every Sun after 3pm ■ www.barcelona.cat/museu-etnologic-culturesmon

The Museum of World Cultures, in the 16th-century Nadal and Marqués de Lló palaces, showcases the cultures of Asia, Africa, America and Oceania. Highlights include Hindu sculptures, Japanese paintings, Nazca ceramics, brass plaques from Benin and Indigenous Australian art.

Museu Etnològic i de Cultures del Món

⑩ El Call

MAP M4 ■ Singagoga Major: C/Marlet 2; 93 317 07 90; adm ■ Centre d'Interpretació del Call: Plaçeta del Manuel Ribé s/n; 93 256 21 22; adm

El Call was home to one of Spain's largest Jewish communities until their expulsion in the 15th century. A few of the original buildings have survived, although a small synagogue (now restored), believed to be one of the oldest in Europe, is on Carrer de Marlet. There is also an interpretation centre dedicated to El Call, run by the city's history museum.

A STROLL THROUGH ROMAN BARCELONA

▶ **MORNING**

Start at the Jaume I metro stop. Walk up Via Laietana to the **Plaça de Ramon Berenguer el Gran** *(see p80)*, which is backed by a stretch of Roman walls. Return to the metro and turn right onto C/Jaume I to get to the **Plaça de Sant Jaume**, the site of the old Roman forum. Leading off to the left is C/Ciutat, which becomes C/Regomir: at No. 3 is **Pati Llimona** *(see p80)*, with an extensive section of Roman walls, one of the four main gateways into the city and the ruins of some thermal baths. There's a good, inexpensive café at Pati Llimona, or you can enjoy some tapas at the **Bodega La Palma** *(see p85)*.

AFTERNOON

Return to the Plaça de Sant Jaume and cross it into tiny C/Paradís, where you'll find vestiges of the **Temple d'August**, a MUHBA site. At the end of the street, turn right and make for the **Plaça del Rei** *(see p46)*. Stop for coffee at the **Café-Bar L'Antiquari** *(see p84)* before visiting the **Museu d'Història de Barcelona** (MUHBA), where you can explore the remains of Roman Barcino. Walk back to C/Comtes, which flanks **Barcelona Cathedral** *(see pp18–19)*, turn right and cross Plaça Nova to C/Arcs, which leads to Avinguda Portal de l'Àngel. Turn left down C/Canuda to reach the **Plaça de la Vila de Madrid** *(see p47)*, where several Roman sarcophagi, found outside the walls according to Roman tradition, are arranged along an old Roman road.

See map on pp76–7 ←

The Best of the Rest

Neo-Gothic bridge, Carrer del Bisbe

1 Carrer del Bisbe
MAP M3

Medieval Carrer del Bisbe is flanked by the Gothic Cases dels Canonges (House of Canons) and the Palau de la Generalitat (see p77). Connecting the two is an eye-catching 1928 Neo-Gothic arched stone bridge.

2 Carrer de Santa Llúcia
MAP M3

This medieval street is home to the Casa de l'Ardiaca (see p19), which features a pretty patio, palm trees and a fountain.

3 Capella de Sant Cristòfol
MAP M4 ▪ C/Regomir 6–8

This chapel dedicated to Sant Cristòfor, the patron saint of travellers, dates from 1503, although it was remodeled in the 1890s. Drivers bring their cars to the chapel annually on the saint's feast day (25 July) to be blessed.

4 Carrer Montcada
MAP P4

The "palace row" of La Ribera is lined with Gothic architectural gems, including the 15th-century Palau Aguilar, which is now home to the Museu Picasso (see pp30–31), and the 17th-century Palau Dalmases with its Gothic chapel, which hosts flamenco performances.

5 Plaça de Ramon Berenguer el Gran
MAP N3

This square is home to one of the largest preserved sections of Barcelona's impressive Roman walls.

6 Carrer Regomir and Carrer del Correu Vell
MAP M5

Find splendid Roman remains on Carrer Regomir, most notably in the medieval Pati Llimona. Two Roman towers can be seen on nearby Carrer del Correu Vell, and there are ruins of Roman walls on the Plaça Traginers.

7 Plaça de Sant Felip Neri
MAP M3

Sunlight filters through tall trees in this hidden oasis of calm. The plaça (see p58) is home to an 18th-century church pocked by bomb damage from the Civil War.

8 Carrer Petritxol
MAP L3

A historic street lined with granges and xocolateries (cafés and chocolate shops). The famous Sala Parés art gallery, which once exhibited Picasso, Casas as well as other Catalan artists, is also located here.

9 Església de Sant Just i Sant Pastor
MAP M4 ▪ Pl de Sant Just s/n ▪ 93 301 74 33 ▪ basilicasantjust.cat

This Gothic church, completed in 1342, has sculptures dating back to the 9th century and 5th-century Visigothic baptismal fonts.

10 Església de Santa Anna
MAP M2 ▪ C/Santa Anna 29 ▪ 93 301 35 76

Mere paces from La Rambla is this tranquil Romanesque church with a leafy 15th-century Gothic cloister.

Remains of Roman Barcino

① MUHBA

Spread beneath MUHBA (see p78) are the extensive remains of Barcino, the Roman settlement that grew into Barcelona. Some sections are remarkably intact, including roads still indented with cart ruts and laundry vats still stained with dye.

② City Entrance Gate
MAP M3 ■ Plaça Nova & Carrer del Bisbe

Towers flanking the entrance to Carrer del Bisbe are the remnants of the only surviving entrance gate to the Roman city, the 4th-century Porta Praetoria.

③ Aqueduct
MAP M3 ■ Plaça Nova & Carrer del Bisbe

Opposite the Porta Praetoria is an archway, part of a reconstructed aqueduct, which would have been one of the several that brought water into the city. In front of it is Joan Brossa's visual poem *Barcino*.

④ Via Sepulcral Romana
MAP M2 ■ Plaça Vila de Madrid ■ Open 11am–2pm Mon, 11am–8pm Tue–Sat (to 7pm Sun) ■ Adm ■ www. barcelona.cat/museuhistoria

The Romans buried their dead in tombs outside the city walls. Several sarcophagi survive in this necropolis, dating from 1st–3rd centuries, and are visible from the walkway spanning the Plaça Vila de Madrid.

Visitors at Via Sepulcral Romana

⑤ Portal del Mar and Baths
MAP M4 ■ Pati Llimona Civic Centre: C/Regomir 3 ■ Open 10am–2pm & 4–6pm Mon–Fri ■ www.pat llimona.net

Travellers and goods brought by ship would pass this gate to enter the city. A bath was obligatory for these travellers and the remnants of the baths can still be seen next to the gate.

⑥ Forum
MAP M4 ■ Plaça Sant Jaume

This large square was the forum and meeting point of the Roman settlement's main arteries: the *cardus* and the *decumanus*.

⑦ Temple d'August
MAP M4 ■ C/Paradís s/n ■ www.barcelona.cat/museuhistoria

An alley just off the Plaça Sant Jaume leads to a quartet of 9-m-(30-ft-) high columns, the only remains of the once-imposing Temple of Augustus from 1st century BC.

⑧ Roman Domus
MAP M4 ■ C/Avinyó 15 ■ Open 10am–2pm Sun ■ Adm ■ www.barcelona.cat/museuhistoria

This Roman house dates between 1st–4th centuries and was discovered in 2004. Parts of the original wall paintings and mosaics can still be seen.

⑨ Walls and Moat
MAP N3 ■ Plaça de Ramón Berenguer el Gran

One of the best-preserved sections of the Roman walls is studded with towers, which have been incorporated into the Plaça de Ramon Berenguer el Gran (see p78).

⑩ Defence Towers
MAP E5 ■ Plaça Traginers

Dating back to the 4th century, this tall, circular watchtower is one of the 78 defensive constructions that once formed part of the Roman walls.

See map on pp76–7 ←

Shops

1 Escribà Confiteria i Fleca
MAP L3 ▪ La Rambla 83
▪ www.escriba.es

If the glistening pastries and towering chocolate creations aren't enough of a lure, then the Modernista storefront certainly is. Buy goodies to go or enjoy them in the café.

2 La Manual Alpargatera
MAP M4 ▪ C/Avinyó 7
▪ Closed Sun ▪ www.lamanual.com

Shoes from La Manual Alpargatera

Notable personalities, including Pope John Paul II, Jack Nicholson and Salvador Dalí, have shopped for *alpargatas* and espadrilles at this famous store.

3 Colmado
MAP P5 ▪ C/Brosoli 5
▪ https://colmadoshop.com

This small boutique has a carefully curated selection of clothing and accessories from stylish labels such as Costa, Heinui and Wolf & Moon.

4 Sombreria Mil
MAP N1 ▪ C/Fontanella 20
▪ Closed Sun ▪ www.sombrereria mil.com

This century-old hat shop offers a fine range of headwear (including the traditional Catalan beret) for men and women.

5 Beatriz Furest
MAP P5 ▪ C/Esparteria 1
▪ Closed Sun ▪ www.beatrizfurest.com

Handcrafted bags and purses by Barcelonian designer Beatriz Furest are sold in this small, chic boutique.

6 Casa Colomina
MAP M3 ▪ C/Cucurulla 2
▪ www.casacolomina.es

Sink your teeth into the Spanish nougat-and-almond speciality *torró*. Casa Colomina, established in 1908, offers a tantalizing array, including chocolate and marzipan varieties.

7 Cereria Subirà
MAP N4 ▪ Baixada Llibreteria 7 ▪ Closed Sun ▪ https://cereria subira.cat

Founded in 1761, this is the city's oldest shop crammed with every kind of candle imaginable.

8 Vila Viniteca
C/Agullers 7 ▪ Closed Sun ▪ www.vilaviniteca.es

This is one of the city's best wine merchants stocking a range of wines and spirits. An adjoining shop sells quality Spanish delicacies, including hams, cheeses and olive oil.

9 Guantería Alonso
MAP M2 ▪ C/Santa Anna 27 ▪ Closed Sun ▪ www.guanteria-alonso.com

This long-established shop is the place to visit for hand-painted fans, handmade gloves, mantillas and other traditional Spanish accessories.

10 L'Arca
MAP M3 ▪ C/Banys Nous 20
▪ https://larcabarcelona.com

Find antique clothing, from flapper dresses to boned corsets, silk shawls, puff-sleeved shirts and wedding dresses here.

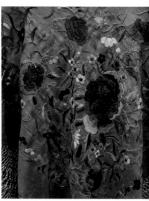

Vintage silk shawl at L'Arca

Cocktail and Conversation Spots

1 Bar L'Ascensor
MAP M4 ■ C/Bellafila 3 ■ 93 318 53 47 ■ Open 6:30pm–1am daily

An old-fashioned, dark-wood elevator serves as the entrance to this dimly lit, convivial bar popular with a cocktail-swilling crowd.

2 Antic Teatre
MAP N2 ■ C/ Verdaguer i Callís 12 ■ Open 10am–11pm Mon–Wed (to midnight Thu & Fri), 5–11pm Sat (to midnight Sun) ■ www.antic teatre.com

This café-bar (see p60) is set in the courtyard of a small theatre. Sit at one of the tables, shaded by trees, for coffee or drinks.

The living-room decor at Milk

3 Milk
MAP M5 ■ C/Gignàs 21 ■ 93 268 09 22 ■ Open 9am–4pm & 7pm–midnight Mon–Fri (to 1:30am Thu & Fri), 9am–5pm & 7pm–1:30am Sat (to midnight Sun)

Decorated like a luxurious living room, Milk serves a lovely brunch (from 9am to 4:30pm), lunch and dinner daily.

4 Las Cuevas de los Rajahs
MAP E5 ■ C/ d'en Cignas 2 ■ Open 7pm–3am Wed–Sat ■ www.lascuevasbar.com

With Neo-Gothic paraphernalia, this bar is set in a cave-like space and offers cocktails, beers and wine.

5 Glaciar
MAP L4 ■ Pl Reial 3 ■ 93 302 1 63 ■ Open 10–2am daily

A café-bar, sought out for the front-row view of the plaça from its terrace.

The 1980s-style Polaroids bar

6 Polaroids
MAP M5 ■ C/Còdols 29 ■ Open 7pm–2:30am daily

A bar with 80s-style decor and retro music, Polaroids offers well-priced drinks that come with free popcorn. Try to arrive early as this place is always packed.

7 La Vinya del Senyor
MAP N5 ■ Pl Santa Maria 5 ■ 93 310 33 79 ■ Opening times vary

Wine lovers from all over the city come here to sample a rich array of Spanish and international varieties.

8 Collage Art & Cocktail Social Club
MAP N5 ■ C/Consellers 4 ■ Open 7pm–2:30am Mon–Sat

Enjoy unique original cocktails at good prices at this spot. The lounge upstairs hosts pocket-size painting exhibitions.

9 Paradiso
MAP F5 ■ C/ de Riera Palau 4 ■ Open 7am–2:30am daily

This cocktail den is accessed speakeasy-style via a gourmet sandwich bar (you need to ask to be let in). The drinks are artistically presented.

10 Mudanzas
MAP P5 ■ C/Vidrieria 15 ■ 933 19 11 37 ■ Open 6pm–2am daily (to 3am Fri & Sat)

With black-and-white tiled floors, and circular marble tables, Mudanzas has a fun, laid-back vibe.

See map on pp76–7 →

Cafés and Light Eats

(1) Mescladís

MAP P3 ▪ C/Carders 35 ▪ 93 295 50 12 ▪ https://mescladis.org ▪ €

This terrace café is run by an NGO that provides culinary training to immigrants. Coffee, drinks and snacks make for an ideal refreshment.

(2) Demásie

MAP F5 ▪ C/de la Princesa 28 ▪ 93 269 11 80 ▪ www.demasie.es

With a bright yellow interior and benches to sit, this bakery serves amazing cakes and cookies. Fresh juices and cold-pressed coffee make this the perfect place for a stopover.

(3) Cafè-Bar L'Antiquari

MAP N4 ▪ C/Veguer 13 ▪ 93 461 95 89

By day, sit by the window and enjoy views of the medieval old town. By night, sip cocktails in the Baroque-inspired upstairs lounge.

(4) Elsa y Fred

MAP F4 & Q2 ▪ C/Rec Comtal 11 ▪ 93 501 66 11 ▪ www.elsayfred.es

With its leather armchairs and big windows, this is the perfect place to enjoy a long, lazy brunch, with dishes ranging from classic *patates braves* to salmon sushi.

(5) Tetería Salterio

MAP M4 ▪ C/Sant Domenec del Call 4 ▪ 93 302 50 28 ▪ Closed Mon–Fri D

Enjoy tea and sweet Arab cakes. Don't miss the *sardo*, a flatbread-style dish with a variety of toppings.

(6) Bistrot Levante

MAP M3 ▪ Placeta de Manuel Ribe ▪ 93 858 2679 ▪ €€

Tuck into babka or avocado toast for breakfast, or kofta and hummus for lunch, at this chic hideaway *(see p64)*. The terrace is perfect on a temperate day.

(7) En Aparté

MAP P2 ▪ C/Lluís el Piadós 2 ▪ 93 269 13 35 ▪ www.enaparte.es

With outside tables overlooking the square, this relaxed café *(see p65)* offers French dishes and wines, good coffee and brunch (Sat and Sun).

(8) Caelum

MAP M3 ▪ C/Palla 8 ▪ 93 302 69 93

Up the stairs of this shop you will find preserves and other foods, all made in Spain's convents and monasteries. Sample the delicacies downstairs at the site of the 15th-century baths.

(9) La Granja Pallaresa

MAP L3 ▪ C/Petritxol 11 ▪ 93 302 20 36

This family-run *xocolateria* has long been serving up thick, dark hot chocolate with *xurros* (fried, sugary dough strips) for dunking.

(10) Bar del Pla

MAP P4 ▪ C/Montcada 2 ▪ 93 268 30 03 ▪ Closed Sun

Savour Spanish tapas with a French twist here. Try the pig's trotters with *foie gras* or the squid ink croquettes.

Entrance to the popular **Bar del Pla**

Restaurants and Tapas Bars

1 Flax & Kale Passage
MAP P2 ■ C/Sant Pere mes Alt 31-33 ■ 93 524 00 52 ■ €€

Part of a small chain of restaurants focusing on healthy, organic food (usually vegan or vegetarian), this venue is tucked down an atmospheric passage.

2 Cal Pep
MAP P5 ■ Pl de les Olles 8 ■ 93 310 79 61 ■ Closed Sun, Mon L, last three weeks of Aug ■ €€

Taste a variety of delicious tapas, including the finest seafood, at this busy, established restaurant.

3 Antic Bocoi
MAP N4 ■ Baixada de Viladecols 4 ■ 93 310 50 57 ■ €€

Delicious Catalan *cocas* (a kind of flat bread) are served with delicious toppings in this lovely spot. There's also a great value set lunch.

4 Casa Delfín
MAP F5 ■ Passeig del Born 36 ■ 93 319 30 88 ■ €€

This pretty bistro uses seasonal produce in imaginative dishes and tapas. The fried artichokes with *romesco* sauce are a must.

5 Llamber
MAP F4 & P4 ■ C/Fusina 5 ■ 93 319 62 50 ■ €€

Enjoy modern Spanish cuisine made with fresh seasonal produce, including homegrown vegetables and Mediterranean red prawns, in a cool, loft-style interior with exposed brickwork and warm woodwork. Also on offer is a wine menu with 30 wines by the glass and 150 by the bottle.

6 Fismuler
MAP Q2 ■ C/Rec Comtal 17 ■ 93 14 00 50 ■ Open L and D daily ■ €€

This relaxed restaurant is known for some of the most inventive and exquisitely presented cuisine in the city. Don't miss the mozzarella salad with leek and hazelnut crumble.

PRICE CATEGORIES

For a three-course meal for one with half a bottle of wine (or equivalent meal), including taxes and extra charges.

€ under €35   €€ €35–50   €€€ over €50

7 Bodega La Palma
MAP M4 ■ Palma de Sant Just 7 ■ 93 315 06 56 ■ Closed Sun ■ €

Set in a former wine cellar, this restaurant offers a delicious choice of tapas, including stuffed Piquillo peppers.

The elegant interior of Rasoterra

8 Rasoterra
MAP M4 ■ C/Palau 5 ■ 93 318 69 26 ■ Closed Sun D, Mon, Tue–Fri L ■ €€

Proponents of the slow food movement, the owners of this stylish, loft-style restaurant serve delicious vegetarian and vegan dishes along with organic wines and beer.

9 El Xampanyet
MAP P4 ■ C/Montcada 22 ■ 93 319 70 03 ■ Closed Sat D, Mon ■ €

An old-fashioned bar popular for its *cava* and range of simple tapas.

10 Govinda
MAP M2 ■ Pl Vila de Madrid 4 ■ 93 318 77 29 ■ Closed Sun–Thu ■ €

A simple restaurant, Govinda serves vegetarian Indian main dishes and delectable desserts, but no alcohol.

See map on pp76–7

🔟 El Raval

The sleek Museu d'Art Contemporani (MACBA) sits near ramshackle tenements; Asian groceries sell spices next to what were once Europe's most decadent brothels; art galleries share narrow streets with smoky old bars – this is a traditional working-class neighbourhood in flux. Since the 1990s it has been undergoing an enthusiastic urban renewal. Although the area has become a magnet for the city's young and hip crowd, it has still got plenty of edge.

Chimney, Palau Güell

EL RAVAL

0 metres 200
0 yards 200

1 Top 10 Sights
see pp86–9

1 Places to Eat
see p93

1 Vintage and Second-Hand Shops see p91

1 Bars
see p92

1 Galleries and Design Shops see p90

The stark white exterior of MACBA

1 Museu d'Art Contemporani (MACBA)

This dramatic, glass-fronted building was designed by American architect Richard Meier. An eclectic array of work by big-name Spanish and international artists is gathered in this contemporary art hub *(see pp34–5)*. Excellent temporary exhibitions display everything from mixed media to sculpture and photography. Opposite stands the Gothic-style 16th-century Convent dels Àngels, built by Bartomeu Roig for the Dominican Tertiary Sisters. This is now used by Capella MACBA for temporary exhibitions, but long-term plans are to extend the galleries and exhibit some of MACBA's collection here permanently.

2 Centre de Cultura Contemporània (CCCB)

Housed in the 18th-century Casa de la Caritat, the CCCB is a focal point for the city's thriving contemporary art scene *(see pp34–5)*. It hosts innovative art exhibitions, literature festivals, film screenings and lectures. A medieval courtyard is dazzlingly offset by a massive angled glass wall, artfully designed to reflect the city's skyline.

3 Museu Marítim

MAP K6 ■ Av de les Drassanes ■ Open 10am–8pm daily ■ Adm, free from 3pm Sun ■ Santa Eulàlia sailing: trip times vary ■ www.mmb.cat

Barcelona's seafaring legacy comes to life at this museum *(see p43)*, located in the beautifully-restored Gothic shipyards. Admire the dramatic Gothic arches, where the royal ships were once built, and the full-scale replica of the *Real*, a 16th-century fighting galley. You can also explore the *Santa Eulàlia (see p102)*, a 1918 schooner moored at the Moll de la Fusta, and even take a sailing trip in her around the seafront (check website for timings and advance booking).

4 Palau Güell

MAP L4 ■ C/Nou de la Rambla 3–5 ■ Open 10am–8pm Tue–Sun (Nov–Mar: to 5:30pm); last entry 1 hr before closing ■ Adm ■ www.palauguell.cat

In 1886, Count Güell asked Gaudí to build him a mansion that would set him apart from his neighbours. The result is the Palau Güell, one of Gaudí's earliest commissions. The interior is darker and less playful than his later works, but stained-glass panels and windows make the most of the light. The rooms are arranged around a huge central salon topped with a domed ceiling. The charming roof terrace hints at the glorious rooftops like La Pedrera.

Sumptuous interior of Palau Güell

5 La Rambla del Raval
MAP K4

This pedestrian walkway, lined with palm trees, started as an attempt by city planners to spark a similar environment to that of the famed La Rambla *(see pp16–17)*. The striking, conical Barceló Hotel, with its panoramic rooftop terrace, and the sleek Filmoteca, a film archive complete with café and cinema, are signs of the area's gentrification. Halfway down the street, Botero's huge, plump bronze *Cat* usually has several neighbourhood kids crawling over its back. Trendy bars and cafés mean the Rambla del Raval rivals its more famous cousin for snacking and people-watching.

6 Avinguda Paral·lel
MAP B3–D5

This long avenue was home to the city's liveliest theatre and cabaret halls at the turn of the 20th century, and, despite being badly bombed in the Civil War, it remains the centre of the theatre district. The area is undergoing a resurgence, spearheaded by the restoration of the landmark El Molino music hall, which dates from 1898. Plans are to open the place as a cultural center after COVID-19 closures. *(see p54)*. The street hosts a number of festivals and there are plans to turn the century-old Teatro Arnau into a museum of the performing arts.

Shop on Carrer de la Riera Baixa

7 Carrers dels Tallers and de la Riera Baixa
MAP L1 & K3

Looking for vintage blue-and-white French navy tops once favoured by the likes of Picasso or bootleg CDs of Madonna's European tour? Along Carrers dels Tallers and de la Riera Baixa in the heart of El Raval are several vintage music and clothing shops selling everything from vinyl records and the latest CDs to original Hawaiian shirts. On Saturdays, Carrer de la Riera Baixa has its own market (open 11am–8:30pm), when its stores display their wares on the street.

8 Filmoteca
MAP K4 ▪ Pl de Salvador Seguí 1–9 ▪ 93 567 10 70 ▪ www.filmoteca.cat

The Filmoteca – the Catalan film archive – occupies a huge, sleek contemporary building just off the Rambla del Raval and has played a large part in the ongoing regeneration of this neighbourhood. It has two screening rooms and shows a varied and interesting programme. This includes film cycles dedicated to the finest directors from around the world, documentaries, Catalan

Buildings on Avinguda Paral·lel

lms, and special events for kids.
's extremely popular, not least
ecause prices are very reasonable.
There is also a great café which has
a library, a documentation centre and
an in-demand outdoor terrace. On
the first Sunday of the month, a flea
market is held in the square outside.

9 Antic Hospital de la Santa Creu

MAP K3 ▪ Entrances on C/Carme
and at C/Hospital 56 ▪ Courtyard:
open 9am–8pm daily

This Gothic hospital complex, now
home to the National Library and
various cultural organizations, dates
from 1401 and is a reminder of the
neighbourhood's medieval past (see
p90). Visitors can wander in a pleasant garden surrounded by Gothic
pillars, but a reader's card is needed
or admission to the library. The
chapel has been converted into a
wonderful contemporary art space.

10 Església de Sant Pau del Camp

MAP J4 ▪ C/Sant Pau 101 ▪ Open
9:30am–noon & 3:30–6:30pm Mon–
Fri, 9:30am–12:30pm Sat; Mass: 8pm
Sat, noon Sun

Deep in the heart of El Raval is this
Romanesque church (see p40), one
of the oldest in Barcelona. Originally
founded as a Benedictine monastery
in the 9th century and subsequently
rebuilt, this ancient church is home
to a 12th-century cloister.

Església de Sant Pau del Camp

A RAMBLE IN EL RAVAL

▶ MORNING

Choose an exhibition that appeals
at either **MACBA** or the **CCCB**
(see p87), the city's two most
important institutions of contemporary art and culture, which sit
right next to each other. Watch
the skateboarders on the **Plaça
dels Àngels** or relax in the café
overlooking the courtyard. Take
C/Joaquin Costa down to the
Rambla del Raval where you can
stroll beneath the palm trees and
admire Fernando Botero's *Cat*.
The Rambla is crammed with
cafés and restaurants: pick one
for lunch, or head to the popular
café in the **Filmoteca**, located
just off the Rambla.

AFTERNOON

At the bottom of the Rambla, turn
right on C/Sant Pau towards the
charming Romanesque monastery of **Església Sant Pau del
Camp**. Admire the simple church
and its miniature cloister with
delicately-carved columns. Then
walk back along C/Sant Pau,
turning right when you reach the
Rambla, then left on C/Nou de la
Rambla. At no. 3 stands Gaudí's
remarkable **Palau Güell** (see p87),
an extravagant mansion that was
one of his first commissions for
the Güells. It has been beautifully
restored, with its lavish salons
and charming rooftop open to
visitors. Kick off the evening with
an absinthe at one of Barcelona's
oldest bars, the **Marsella** (see
p92), before heading to the
nearby **Bar Muy Buenas** (see
p92), which is decorated with
Modernista detailings.

See map on p86

Galleries and Design Shops

(1) Galeria dels Àngels
MAP L2 ▪ C/Pintor Fortuny 27 ▪ Open 10:30am–7pm Mon–Sat ▪ https://angelsbarcelona.com

Works of emerging and established artists are showcased at this painting, photography and sculpture gallery.

(2) Miscelanea
MAP K5 ▪ C/Dr Dou 16 ▪ Open 11:30am–8:30pm Mon–Sat ▪ www.miscelanea.info

Miscelanea is an artists' project. It is a multifunctional space, with a gallery for exhibitions featuring works by emerging artists, a shop selling design objects and a café.

***Fish*, Imanol Ossa**

(3) Siesta
MAP K2 ▪ C/Ferlandina 18 ▪ Open 11am–2pm & 5–8:30pm Mon–Fri ▪ https://siestaweb.com

Part boutique, part art gallery, Siesta sells unique ceramics, jewellery and glass art. It also hosts exhibitions.

(4) MACBA Store Laie
MAP K2 ▪ Plaça dels Àngels 1 ▪ Open Fri–Sun ▪ www.macba.cat/en/visit/store-library

This museum bookshop has a range of designer gifts, including stationery, homeware, toys and games as well as books on art.

(5) Grey Street
MAP D4 ▪ C/Peu de la Creu 25 ▪ Open 11am–3pm & 4–8pm Mon–Sat ▪ www.greystreetbarcelona.com

This lovingly curated shop sells mostly locally made gifts and crafts, from stationery to jewellery and bags.

(6) HeyShop
MAP L2 ▪ C/Dr Dou 4 ▪ Open 11am–7pm Mon–Sat (to 8pm Sat) ▪ www.heyshop.es

Design and illustration studio stocking prints, notebooks, T-shirts and more.

(7) Imanol Ossa
MAP D4 & K2 ▪ C/Peu de la Creu 24 ▪ www.imanolossa.com

Lamps, jewellery, and mobiles are made from all kinds of upcycled treasures at this studio run by a young designer. Call for opening hours.

(8) Fantastik
MAP K1 ▪ C/Joaquin Costa 62 ▪ 93 301 30 68 ▪ Open 11am–2pm & 4–8:30pm Mon–Sat

A colourful array of covetable items from around the world, including bright Mexican fabrics and rugs from India, are available at affordable prices.

(9) La Capella
MAP K3 ▪ C/Hospital 56 ▪ Opening times vary, check website ▪ lacapella.barcelona/ca

This Gothic chapel at the Antic Hospital de la Santa Creu *(see p89)* is now a contemporary art gallery *(see p70)* run by the city and dedicated to emerging artists.

The Gothic La Capella gallery

(10) Room Service
MAP E4 ▪ C/dels Àngels 16 ▪ Open 11am–2pm Mon–Fri ▪ www.roomsd.com

This commercial gallery is dedicated to cutting-edge design, principally for the home. International creators are represented, along with up-and-coming local talent.

Vintage and Second-Hand Shops

The vibrant interior of Holala Ibiza

① Holala Ibiza
MAP L1 ▪ C/Tallers 73 ▪ 933 02
05 93 ▪ Open noon–3pm & 5–8pm
Mon–Sat

Rummage for an outfit at this three-floor vintage store, with everything from silk kimonos to army pants and colourful 1950s bathing suits.

② Flamingos
MAP D4 & K2 ▪ C/de Ferlandina
20 ▪ 93 182 43 87 ▪ Open noon–8pm
Mon–Sat

This vintage store, also selling old posters and bric-a-brac, operates on a weight system: you pay per kilo, depending on the clothing category.

③ Fusta'm
MAP K1 ▪ C/Joaquim Costa 62
▪ 639 527 076 ▪ Open 11am–2pm &
4–8pm Mon–Fri

Discover second-hand furniture, lighting and decorative objects from around the world in the style of the 1950s, 60s and 70s, all completely restored at the store's workshop.

④ Revólver Records
MAP L2 ▪ C/Tallers 11 ▪ 93 412
73 58 ▪ Open 10am–9pm Mon–Sat

The speciality here is classic rock, and the wall art fittingly depicts The Rolling Stones and Jimi Hendrix. One floor houses CDs, the other vinyl.

⑤ Wilde Sunglasses Store
MAP K2 ▪ C/Joaquin Costa 2
▪ Open 1–8pm Mon–Sat

This dimly-lit boudoiresque boutique is lined with vintage-style sunglasses, that range from aviator shades to pairs of cat's-eye specs.

⑥ Holala Plaça
MAP L1 ▪ Pl Castella 2
▪ 933 02 05 93 ▪ Open 11am–
9pm Mon–Sat

This huge shop sells second-hand clothes, furniture and bric-a-brac.

⑦ La Principal Retro & Co
MAP K1 ▪ C/Valldonzella 52
▪ 60 726 57 57 ▪ Open noon–
3pm & 4–8pm Mon–Sat

Set in a charming old dairy, this chic boutique has a lovely range of vintage clothing for men and women.

⑧ Soul BCN
MAP L1 ▪ C/Tallers 15
▪ 93 481 32 94 ▪ Open 11am–
8:30pm Mon–Sat

A vintage-style shop, Soul BCN sells 1950s frocks, cat's-eye sunglasses, flirty Bardot tops and much more.

⑨ Discos Tesla
MAP L2 ▪ C/Tallers 3 ▪ 664
095 091 ▪ Open 10am–8:30pm
Mon–Sat

This record and CD store focuses on alternative music from decades past. Visitors can hum a few lines of a song and the owner will track it down.

⑩ Lullaby
MAP D4 ▪ C/Riera Baixa 22
▪ 93 443 08 02

You will find all sorts of treasures in this quirky little boutique, from floaty frocks to vintage sportswear, along with some fabulous jewellery and handbags.

See map on p86

Bars

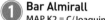
Bar Almirall, founded in 1860

1 Bar Almirall
MAP K2 ▪ C/Joaquin Costa 33
▪ Opening times vary, check website
▪ www.casaalmirall.com

Founded in 1860, the city's oldest bar retains many original fittings and has eclectic music and strong cocktails.

2 El Jardí
MAP K3 ▪ C/Hospital 56
▪ 93 681 92 34 ▪ Open 1–11pm daily

Escape the crowds in this peaceful outdoor café-bar (see p60), overlooking a garden. Go for the *vermut* (see p65) and some olives.

3 La Confitería
MAP J4 ▪ C/Sant Pau 2
▪ Opening times vary, check website ▪ www.confiteria.cat

Set in a former sweet shop, this bar has original Modernista fittings. Tasty cocktails and tapas are on the menu.

4 Marsella
MAP K4 ▪ C/Sant Pau 65
▪ Open 5pm–midnight Mon–Thu & Sun (to 1am Fri–Sat)

A dimly lit Modernista bar, Marsella serves cocktails and absinthe to regulars and first-timers.

5 Two Shmucks
MAP K2 ▪ C/Joaquín Costa 52
▪ 674 480 073

This buzzy neighbourhood bar made it on to the 50 Best Bars in the world. Every night has a different theme, and the imaginative cocktail menu changes regularly.

6 Betty Ford's
MAP K1 ▪ C/Joaquin Costa 56 ▪ 93 304 13 68 ▪ Open 5pm–12:30am (to 3am Fri & Sat)

Named after the Hollywood set's favourite rehab and detox centre, this cocktail bar has a 1950s vibe.

7 Bar Kasparo
MAP L2 ▪ Pl Vicenç Martorell 4 ▪ Open 9am–midnight daily ▪ www.kasparo.es

During the day, this charming bar (see p60) is a favourite with families, but come dusk it's a fabulous place to chill out over a glass of wine.

8 Boadas Cocktail Bar
MAP L2 ▪ C/Tallers 1 ▪ Open noon–1:30am Tue–Sat ▪ www.boadascocktails.com

Founded in 1933, Boadas continues to mix the best martinis in town.

9 Bar Palosanto
MAP K4 ▪ Rambla de Raval 26 ▪ Open 6–11:30pm Mon, Thu–Sun

A colourful café-bar with a few outdoor tables, this is a cosy spot for drinks, tapas and light meals.

10 Bar Muy Buenas
MAP D4 ▪ C/del Carme 63
▪ Opening noon–midnight daily
▪ www.muybuenas.cat ▪ €

A Modernista-era bar, Muy Buenas serves spirits and wine made in Catalonia along with refined tapas and Catalan classics.

Modernista decor at Bar Muy Buenas

Places to Eat

1 Caravelle
MAP E4 ■ C/Pintor Fortuny 31 ■ 93 317 98 92 ■ Closed D daily ■ €

This spot near the MACBA museum has become a favourite for weekend brunch and long coffee breaks. The menu changes regularly but is likely to include delicious huevos rancheros and vegetarian options.

2 Superclàssic
MAP D4 ■ C/Floristes de la Rambla 14 ■ 93 197 78 29 ■ €

On offer at this friendly spot are a mix of classic and more inventive tapas, including several veggie and vegan options. Grab a seat on the terrace overlooking the square.

3 La Esquina
MAP E3 ■ C/Bergara 2 ■ www. laesquinabarcelona.com ■ €

A spacious café, La Esquina serves delicious all-day brunch and light lunch fare such as pulled pork tacos and Caeser salad.

4 Bacaro
MAP L3 ■ C/Jerusalén 6 ■ 672 17 60 68 ■ Closed Sun ■ www. bacarobarcelona.com ■ €€

Tucked behind the Boqueria market, this convivial little Italian restaurant-bar serves modern Venetian cuisine.

5 Biocenter
MAP L2 ■ C/Pintor Fortuny 25 ■ 93 301 45 83 ■ Opening times vary ■ www.restaurantebiocenter.es ■ €

At this vegetarian restaurant, dishes are prepared with organic produce. There's an array of dishes to choose from, including amazing desserts (vegan, gluten-free and sugar-free options are available).

6 A Tu Bola
MAP D4 ■ C/de Hospital 78 ■ 93 315 32 44 ■ Closed Tue ■ €€

A local favourite, A Tu Bola is well known for its fish, meat and vege-table balls served between bread with a range of dips and sauces.

PRICE CATEGORIES

For a three-course meal for one with half a bottle of wine (or equivalent meal), including taxes and extra charges.

€ under €35   €€ €35–50   €€€ over €50

7 Teresa Carles
MAP L1 ■ C/Jovellanos 2 ■ 93 317 18 29 ■ https://teresacarles.com ■ €

Come here for imaginative vegetarian fare, such as crêpes with artichokes and brie. It's the flagship of a small chain of healthy food restaurants.

Fresh salad served at Teresa Carles

8 Cera 23
MAP J3 ■ C/Cera 23 ■ 93 442 0808 ■ Open 7:30–11pm Fri–Tue ■ €€

A stylish Galician restaurant, Cera 23 serves northern Spain's classic dishes with a contemporary twist.

9 Els Ocellets
MAP D4 ■ Ronda Sant Pau 55 ■ Closed Sun D, Mon, late Jul–late Aug ■ €

Traditional cuisine with a creative touch in elegant surroundings. Good value fixed-price menus.

10 L'Havana
MAP K2 ■ C/Lleó 1 ■ 93 302 21 06 ■ Closed Sun D, Mon, 4 weeks in Jul–Aug ■ €€

This restaurant serves superb Catalan cuisine. Try the fresh fish of the day or classic dishes such as pig's trotters.The set lunch menu is excellent too.

See map on p86

TOP 10 Montjuïc

Named the "Jewish Mountain" after an important Jewish cemetery that existed here in the Middle Ages, this sizable park was first landscaped for the 1929 International Exhibition, when the Palau Nacional and the Mies van der Rohe Pavilion were also built. However, the area soon fell into general disuse, becoming synonymous with decline. With the grim shadow left by the castle, which for years acted as a slaughterhouse for Franco's firing squads, it is little short of miraculous that Montjuïc is now one of the city's biggest draws. As the site for the 1992 Olympics, it was transformed into a beautiful green oasis, with fabulous museums and sports facilities all connected by a network of outdoor escalators and interlaced with quiet, shady gardens.

Statue, Castell de Montjuïc

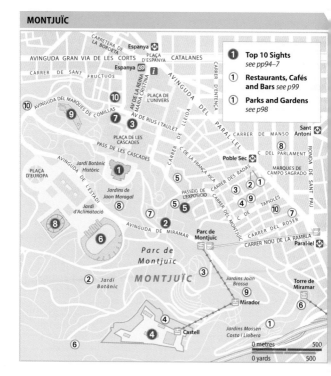

MONTJUÏC

1 **Top 10 Sights**
see pp94–7

1 **Restaurants, Cafés and Bars** see p99

1 **Parks and Gardens** see p98

1 Palau Nacional and Museu Nacional d'Art de Catalunya

The Palau Nacional is home to the Museu Nacional d'Art de Catalunya (see pp20–21), which exhibits Catalonia's historic art collections. Home to one of Europe's finest displays of Romanesque art, the museum includes a series of 12th-century frescoes, rescued from Catalan Pyrenean churches and painstakingly reassembled in a series of galleries.

2 Fundació Joan Miró

One of Catalonia's most acclaimed painters and sculptors, Joan Miró (1893–1983) donated many of the 11,000 works held by the museum. Housed in a stark white building designed by his friend, architect Josep Lluís Sert, this (see p28–9) is the world's most complete collection of Miró's work.

3 Font Màgica

MAP B4 ■ Pl Carles Buigas 1 (off Av Reina Maria Cristina) ■ Shows: Apr, May & first 2 weeks of Oct: 9pm & 9:30pm Thu–Sat; Jun–Sep: 9:30pm & 10pm Wed–Sun; mid-Dec–Mar: 8pm & 9pm Thu–Sat; mid-Oct–mid-Dec: no shows

Below the cascades and fountains that decend from the Palau Nacional is the Magic Fountain (see p70), designed by Carles Buigas for the International Exhibition of 1929. As darkness falls, countless jets of water are choreographed in

Font Màgica's soaring jets of water

a mesmerizing sound and light show. When the water meets in a single jet it can soar to 15 m (50 ft). The finale is often accompanied by a recording of Freddie Mercury and soprano Montserrat Caballé singing the anthem *Barcelona* as the water fades from pink to green and back to white. The Four Columns behind the fountain represent the Catalan flag and are a symbol of the Catalanism movement.

4 Castell de Montjuïc

MAP B6 ■ Carretera de Montjuïc 66 ■ Open 10am–6pm daily (Apr–Oct: to 8pm) ■ Adm ■ https://ajuntament.barcelona.cat/castelldemontjuic

Dominating Montjuïc's hill, this castle was once a prison and torture centre for political prisoners. At the end of the Spanish Civil War, 4,000 Catalan nationalists and republicans were shot in the nearby Fossar de la Pedrera. The museum explores the history of Montjuïc, as well as the role of the castle in the Civil War. Visitors can still climb the fort's bastions for superb views of the port below.

Castell de Montjuïc

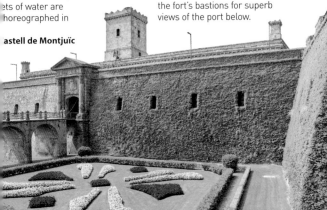

The atmospheric Teatre Grec

5 Teatre Grec

MAP C4 ■ Pg Santa Madrona
■ Open 10am–dusk daily ■ Adm for
shows ■ www.barcelona.cat/grec

This beautiful amphitheatre *(see p54)*
was inspired by the Classical ideas of
what was known as *Noucentisme*. This
late 19th-century Catalan architectural
movement was a reaction to the overly-
decorative nature of *Modernisme*.
With its leafy green backdrop and
beautiful gardens, there are few places
more enchanting than this to enjoy
an afternoon's stroll, watch *Swan
Lake* or listen to some jazz. The
open-air theatre is used for shows
during the summertime Grec Festival
(see p73), when it also becomes home
to a luxurious outdoor restaurant.

6 Estadi Olímpic

MAP B5 ■ Av de l'Estadi 60
■ Museum: open 10am–6pm Tue–
Sat, 10am–2:30pm Sun ■ Adm for
museum ■ www.estadiolimpic.
barcelona

The stadium was first built for the
1936 Workers' Olympics, which were
cancelled with the outbreak of the
Spanish Civil War *(see pp38–9)*. The
original Neo-Classical façade is still

in place, but the stadium was rebuilt
for the 1992 Olympic Games *(see
p39)*. The interactive Museu Olímpic
de l'Esport nearby is dedicated to all
aspects of sport. You can also view
the stadium from the upper levels.

7 Pavelló Mies van der Rohe

MAP B4 ■ Av Francesc Ferrer i
Guàrdia 7 ■ Open 10am–8pm
daily (Nov–Feb: to 6pm) ■ Adm (free
for under 16s) ■ https://miesbcn.com

You might wonder exactly what this
box-like pavilion of stone, marble,
onyx and glass is doing in the middle
of Montjuïc's monumental architecture. This architectural gem was
Germany's contribution to the 1929
International Exhibition. Built by
Ludwig Mies van der Rohe (1886–
1969), the Rationalist pavilion was
soon demolished, only to be reconstructed in 1986. Inside, the sculpture
Morning by Georg Kolbe (1877–1947)
is reflected in a small lake.

8 Palau Sant Jordi

MAP A4 ■ Pg Olímpic 5–7
■ Open 10am–6pm Sat & Sun
■ www.palausantjordi.barcelona

The biggest star of all the Olympic
facilities is this steel-and-glass indoor
stadium (closed to the public) and
multipurpose installation designed
by Japanese architect Arata Isozaki.
Holding around 17,000 people, the
stadium is the home of the city's
basketball team. The esplanade –
a surreal forest of concrete and
metal pillars – was designed by Aiko
Isozaki, Arata's wife. Further down
the hill are the indoor and outdoor
Bernat Picornell Olympic pools, both
of which are open to the public.

Palau Sant Jordi

⑨ Poble Espanyol

MAP A3 ■ Av Francesc Ferrer i Guàrdia ■ Open 9am–8pm Mon, 9am–midnight Tue–Thu & Sun, 9am–3am Fri, 9am–4pm Sat ■ Adm ■ www. poble-espanyol.com

This Spanish *poble* (village) features famous buildings and streets from around Spain recreated in full-scale. Poble Espanyol has become a centre for arts and crafts, including an impressive glass-blowers' workshop, and is one of the city's most popular attractions. There are many shops selling local crafts and also plenty of restaurants and cafés.

Traditional alleys of Poble Espanyol

⑩ CaixaForum

MAP B3 ■ Av Francesc Ferrer i Guàrdia 6–8 ■ Open 10am–8pm daily ■ Adm ■ https://caixaforum.es

The Fundació La Caixa's impressive collection of contemporary art is housed in a former textile factory built in 1911 by Catalan Modernista architect Puig i Cadafalch. Restored and opened as a gallery in 2002, it assembles almost 800 works by Spanish and foreign artists, shown in rotation along with temporary international exhibitions. The roof terrace offers great views of the city.

A DAY IN MONTJUÏC

▶ MORNING

To get to the **Fundació Joan Miró** *(see pp28–9)* before the crowds and with energy to spare, hop on the funicular from Paral·lel metro station. It is a short walk from the funicular to the museum, where you'll need an hour and a half to absorb the impressive collection of Miró paintings, sketches and sculptures. When you've had your fill of contemporary art, refuel with a *cafè amb llet (see p65)* on the restaurant terrace before backtracking along Av de Miramar and jumping on the cable car up to **Castell de Montjuïc** *(see p95)*. Wander the castle gardens and look out over the city and the bustling docks. Return to Av de Miramar by cable car and pop back in to the Miró Foundation for a simple lunch at the café (note there aren't many eating options in Montjuïc). Then follow signs for MNAC in the **Palau Nacional** *(see p95)*.

AFTERNOON

After lunch, spend time admiring the extraordinary Romanesque art collection at **MNAC** *(see pp20–21)*. When you exit, turn right and follow the signs to the Olympic complex. The **Estadi Olímpic** is worth a look, but the silver-domed **Palau Sant Jordi** steals the limelight. Spend the late afternoon cooling down with a dip in the fantastic open-air pool at nearby Bernat Picornell. From here it is a short stroll to the **Poble Espanyol,** where you can settle in at a terrace bar in Plaça Major.

See map on p94

Parks and Gardens

1 Jardins Mossèn Costa i Llobera

MAP C5 ▪ Open 10am–dusk daily

These are among Europe's most important cactus and succulent gardens. They are particularly impressive as the sun sets, when surreal shapes and shadows emerge.

2 Jardí Botànic

MAP A5 ▪ Open Apr–Sep: 10am–8pm daily; Oct–Mar: 10am–5pm daily ▪ Adm (free first Sun of month, every Sun after 3pm) ▪ https://museuciencies.cat

Barcelona's botanical gardens are found among the stadiums used in the Olympics of 1992. Dating from 1999, the gardens contain hundreds of examples of typical Mediterranean flora. Don't miss the charming Jardí Botànic Històric nearby (see p71).

3 Jardins Mossèn Cinto Verdaguer

MAP C5 ▪ Open 10am–dusk daily

The best time to visit these wonderfully elegant gardens is during spring, when the plants are in blossom and the colours and scents are in full force.

4 Jardins del Castell

MAP B5

Cannons dotted among the rose bushes and pathways along the walls of a flower-filled moat are the highlights of these gardens which ring the castle.

5 Jardins del Teatre Grec

MAP C4

Reminiscent of the Hanging Gardens of Babylon, this gracious oasis surrounding the Greek amphitheatre is officially known as La Rosadela.

6 Jardins de Miramar

MAP C5

Opposite the Miramar hotel, these gardens are scattered with stairways leading to leafy groves with vistas across the city and the port area.

7 Jardins Laribal

MAP B4 ▪ Open 10am–dusk daily

This multilevel park hides a small Modernista house by architect Puig i Cadafalch and the Font del Gat, a drinking fountain which has inspired many local songs.

8 Jardins de Joan Maragall

MAP B4 ▪ Open 10am–3pm Sat & Sun

An avenue lined with sculptures by Frederic Marès and Ernest Maragall is the main delight in the Jardins de Joan Maragall, which also has the last of the city's *ginjoler* trees.

A sculpture at Joan Brossa gardens

9 Jardins de Joan Brossa

MAP C5 ▪ Open 10am–dusk daily

The variety of grasses and trees alone make Joan Brossa gardens truly fascinating. A cross between city gardens and a woodland park, these gardens come into their own in spring, but are popular all year – thanks to the musical instruments, climbing frames and a flying fox.

10 El Mirador del Llobregat

MAP A3

A viewing area with small gardens nearby, this is the only place in the city where you can see the plains of the Llobregat stretching below.

Restaurants, Cafés and Bars

PRICE CATEGORIES
For a three-course meal for one with half a bottle of wine (or equivalent meal), including taxes and extra charges.

€ under €35 ■ €€ €35–50 ■ €€€ over €50

The stylish La Caseta del Migdia

1 Malabida
MAP C4 ■ C/Blai 63 ■ 93 175 81 79 ■ Closed Sun and Mon ■ €
A welcoming spot, Malabida offers simple tapas, tasty sandwiches and platters of cheese and charcuterie.

2 Mano Roto
MAP C4 ■ C/Creu dels Molers 4 ■ 93 164 80 41 ■ Closed Mon–Fri D ■ www.manorota.net ■ €€€
The seasonal dishes at this stylish bistro are a creative fusion of Catalan, Japanese and Peruvian cuisines.

3 El Sortidor
MAP C4 ■ Pl del Sortidor 5 ■ 690 765 721 ■ Closed Mon ■ €
Featuring original stained-glass doors and tiled floors from 1908, El Sortidor serves meals in a romantic setting.

4 La Tomaquera
MAP C4 ■ C/Margarit 58 ■ 675 902 389 ■ Closed Sun D, Mon, Aug & Easter week ■ €
Gorge on delicious Catalan home food at bargain prices at this restaurant. The snails served here are considered the best in town.

5 El Lliure
MAP B4 ■ Pg Santa Madrona 40-46 ■ 664 862 623 ■ Closed Mon–Fri D, Sat L (except on days with performances) ■ €
The Lliure theatre has a café with an adjoining restaurant and terrace area. Ideal for having a meal before a show.

6 La Caseta del Migdia
MAP B6 ■ Mirador del Migdia ■ Closed Apr–Sep: Mon & Tue; Oct–Mar: Mon–Fri ■ €
Leave the city behind and head for this lofty outdoor bar (see p60) at the top of Montjuïc, where you can enjoy ice-cold drinks, a welcome breeze and amazing views.

7 La Federica
MAP D4 ■ C/de Salvà 3 ■ 93 600 59 01 ■ Closed Sun & Mon ■ €
A vintage-style bar, La Federica serves brunch as well as tasty and imaginative tapas to go with a wide range of cocktails.

8 Bar Calders
MAP C4 ■ C/Parlament 25 ■ 93 329 93 49 ■ Closed Mon–Thu L ■ €
This sought-after terrace spot (see p61) is ideal for relaxing over a vermut (see p65) or an expertly mixed gin and tonic.

9 O Meu Lar
MAP C4 ■ C/Margarit 24 ■ 93 329 70 74 ■ Closed Sun ■ €€
A traditional Galician restaurant lined with old photos. The specialities here are tapas and charcoal-grilled meats.

10 Quimet & Quimet
MAP C4 ■ C/Poeta Cabanyes 25 ■ 93 442 31 42 ■ Closed Sat, Sun & three weeks in Aug ■ €
This tiny bodega has standing room only, but serves delicious tapas and wonderful wines.

See map on p94

🔟 The Seafront

The azure waters of the Mediterranean are only ever a few metro stops away. The city's beaches were once hidden behind an industrial wasteland, but things changed radically in preparation for the 1992 Olympics. The plan was to create

Statue, Parc de la Ciutadella

a city *oberta al mar* (open to the sea); the result is phenomenal. Sandy beaches and shady palm trees now stretch from Barceloneta to the yacht-filled Port Olímpic and beyond. Behind it is Poblenou, a once humble neighbourhood that has been transformed and is now a hub for tech companies and design studios. Just inland, the leafy expanse of the Parc de la Ciutadella, with its fountain and boating lake, is the perfect green retreat.

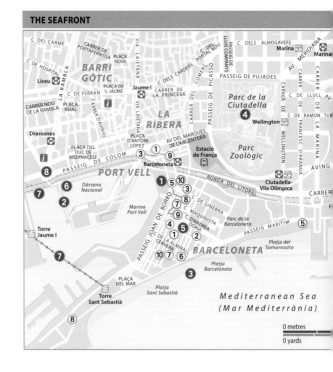

THE SEAFRONT

1 Museu d'Història de Catalunya

MAP N6 ▪ Pl Pau Vila 3 ▪ Open 10am–7pm Tue–Sat (to 8pm Wed), 10am–2:30pm Sun ▪ Adm; free first Sun of the month ▪ www.mhcat.cat

Housed in the Palau de Mar, a renovated portside warehouse, this museum *(see p53)* offers a broad, interactive exploration of Catalonia's history since prehistoric times. Kids especially will have a ball with the engaging exhibits, such as a Civil War-era bunker and a recreated Catalan bar from the 1960s with an ancient *futbolín* (table football) game.

2 Rambla de Mar

MAP E5 ▪ Moll d'Espanya ▪ Maremagnum: open 10am–10pm daily

Saunter along the Rambla de Mar, a floating wooden pier that leads to the flashy Maremagnum

The floating Rambla de Mar pier

mall. It is open every day of the year, which makes it particularly popular with shoppers on Sundays.

3 Beaches

MAP E6

If a splash in the Mediterranean interests you, head down to the end of La Rambla, wander along the palm tree-lined Moll de la Fusta, and down the restaurant-packed Passeig Joan de Borbó where the sea beckons. More than 7 km (4.3 miles) of blue-flag beaches stretch north from Barceloneta to Port Olímpic and beyond. The seawater quality can vary, depending on the tides. Facilities are top-notch, including showers, deck chairs, lifeguards and beach volleyball courts. The beachfront boardwalk is the perfect spot for a stroll. Look out for Rebecca Horn's beautiful sculpture, *L'Estel Ferit* (The Wounded Star), a local landmark.

4 Parc de la Ciutadella

MAP R4 ▪ Pg Pujades ▪ Open 10am–10:30pm daily; zoo timings vary ▪ Zoo: adm

Colourful parrots take flight from the top of palm trees and orange groves dotted around this famous park. A perfect picnic spot, the city's largest central green space *(see p48)* is particularly popular on Sunday after-noons when people gather to play instruments, relax, head out onto the boating lake for a punt, or visit the museum and the zoo. The north-eastern corner of the park features a magnificent fountain – a cascading waterfall topped by a chariot rider flanked by griffins caught mid-roar.

Old buildings of Barceloneta

5 Barceloneta
MAP F5

A portside warren of narrow streets, small squares and ancient bars, this traditional neighbourhood of *pescadors* (fishermen) and *mariners* (sailors) seems worlds apart from the mega-malls and disco lights of nearby Port Olímpic. A refreshing foray through this tight-knit community yields a glimpse into the Barcelona of 150 years ago. Older couples still pull chairs out onto the street to gossip and watch the world go by, and small seafood restaurants serve a *menú del dia* of whatever is fresh off the boat. Running the length of Barceloneta's western edge is the Passeig Joan de Borbó, which is lined with restaurants serving *mariscs* (shellfish) and paellas.

6 Pailebot Santa Eulàlia
MAP L6 ■ Moll de la Fusta ■ Opening times vary, check website ■ Adm ■ www.mmb.cat

Bobbing in the water at the Moll de la Fusta (Timber Quay) is this restored three-mast schooner, originally christened *Carmen Flores*. It first set sail from Spain in 1918. On journeys to Cuba, the ship used to transport textiles and salt, returning with tobacco, coffee, cereals and wood. In 1997, the Museu Marítim *(see p87)* bought and restored the ship as part of a project to create a collection of sea-worthy historical Catalan vessels.

7 Boat and Cable-Car Trips
MAP E5/6 ■ Telefèric: from Torre San Sebastià ■ Las Golondrinas: Portal de la Pau ■ Approximately every 30 mins from 11:15am ■ https://lasgolondrinas.com ■ Orsom: Portal de la Pau; https://barcelona-orsom.com ■ For timings call 667 592 306 ■ barcelona-orsom.com

Observe all the activity at Barcelona's bustling port area from a different perspective, either from the air or the sea. The *Transbordador Aeri* cable cars offer sweeping bird's-eye views of Barcelona and its coast, while the old-fashioned Las Golondrinas "swallow boats" and the Orsom Catamaran make regular sight-seeing trips around the harbour, the beaches and the port area.

8 Monument a Colom
MAP E5

This 60-m- (197-ft-) high column was built between 1882 and 1888 for Barcelona's Universal Exhibition and commemorates Christopher Columbus's first voyage to the Americas; it was in Barcelona that Columbus met Ferdinand and Isabel on his return. Columbus stands on top of the column *(see p16)*, pointing out to sea, supposedly towards the New World but actually towards Italy. There have been calls by some to have the statue removed; Mayor Ada Colau has pushed back, stating the city should own up to its past rather than deny it and keep the statue as a reminder.

9 Poblenou and Palo Alto Design Complex

MAP H5 ▪ www.poblenouurbandis trict.com/en ▪ www.paloalto.barcelona

The fashionable Poblenou district has become a hub for startups and tech companies. A burgeoning number of trendy cafés and shops have opened, bold contemporary buildings are sprouting up and the old industrial warehouses are being restored and repurposed. One contains BD Design, the city's most prestigious design showroom, while the Palo Alto complex houses the studios of big-name designers.

10 Museu de Ciències Naturals

Pl Leonardo da Vinci 4–5, Parc del Fòrum ▪ 93 256 60 02 ▪ Opening times vary, check website ▪ Adm; free first Sun of the month, every Sun after 3pm ▪ https://museuciencies.cat

The main site of the Museu de Ciències Naturals occupies a raised triangular building constructed by Herzog & de Meuron for Barcelona's Forum 2004 event. This is a great, family-friendly place, with an appeal-ing mix of contemporary exhibits and old-fashioned cabinets full of stuffed animals. The main exhibition is a "biography of the earth", with inter-active audiovisual displays about "the origins of the world. There is a special area for the under-7s to learn about science, plus a library and café. The Jardí Botànic (see p98) is also part of the Museu de Ciències Naturals.

Museu de Ciències Naturals

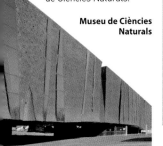

See map on pp100–101

EXPLORING THE PORT

▶ **MORNING**

Begin your port *passeig* (stroll) with a visit to the **Museu Marítim** (see p87), where you can sense Barcelona's status as one of the most active ports in the Mediterranean. From here, head towards the Monument a Colom and stroll along the Moll de la Fusta to admire the **Pailebot Santa Eulàlia**, which has been meticulously restored by the museum. Take a stroll down the **Rambla de Mar** (see p101), an undulating wooden drawbridge that leads to the **Maremagnum** (see p67) shopping mall. At the start of the pier, take a boat ride on the Orsom Catamaran, where you can grab a drink and a snack. Soak up the sunshine and the port skyline while sprawled out on a net just inches above the water. Back on land, stroll down the Moll d'Espanya and turn towards the traditional fisher's quarter of **Barceloneta**, an atmospheric pocket of narrow streets and timeworn bars. Get a real taste of old-style Barcelona at the boisterous tapas place, **El Vaso de Oro** (C/Balboa 6). Head to the bar and savour tasty seafood.

AFTERNOON

Head to Passeig Joan de Borbó and the beach. Douse yourself in the Med, then siesta in the afternoon sun. Pick yourself up with sangria at the beach-side **Salamanca** *xiringuito* (at the end of Pg Joan de Borbó), where you can watch the waves lap the shore as the sun dips below the horizon.

Bars and Tapas Bars

Lively *xiringuitos* on Mar Bella

1 Mar Bella beach bars
Platja Nova Mar Bella ▪ Closed winters

Head to one of the *xiringuitos* (beach bars) found on Barcelona's hippest beach and enjoy the DJ sessions.

2 Xiringuito Escribà
Av Litoral 62, Platja de Bogatell ▪ www.restaurantsescriba.com

A beach bar right on the sand, this spot offers breakfast, tapas, light meals, cocktails and more.

3 Bar Jai Ca
MAP F5 ▪ C/Ginebra 13 ▪ www.barjaica.com

This is a relaxed neighbourhood favourite. Delicious tapas and good wine are on offer.

4 Bodega Fermín
MAP F6 ▪ C/Sant Carles 18 ▪ Open noon–midnight Sun–Thu (to 1am Fri–Sat)

Laidback hangout, with craft beers on tap and a great choice of simple, tasty tapas. It's a great place to enjoy a *vermut*, the preferred aperitif.

5 Eclipse
MAP F6 ▪ W Hotel, Pl de la Rosa dels Vents 1 ▪ www.eclipse-barcelona.com

The spectacular bar on the 26th floor of the W Hotel (commonly known as the Hotel Vela) offers lovely views of the city. Smart dress code.

6 Bus Terraza
Parc del Fòrum, Avda del Litoral 488 ▪ Opening times vary ▪ www.busterraza.com

There are regular DJ sessions and live jazz concerts at this converted double-decker bus (*see p61*).

7 L'Òstia
MAP F6 ▪ Plaça de la Barceloneta ▪ www.lostiabcn.com

A modern take on a classic tavern, this spot serves a fine array of traditional tapas as well as fresh seafood, which you can enjoy on the charming terrace.

8 La Bombeta
MAP F6 ▪ C/Maquinista 33 ▪ 93 319 94 45

This popular Catalan bar offers a wonderful glimpse of life in Barcelona before the tourists arrived. The house speciality is the *bombas*, deep-fried balls of mashed potatoes served with a spicy meat-and-tomato sauce. Be prepared to wait for a table.

9 Can Ganassa
MAP F6 ▪ Pl de la Barceloneta 4–6 ▪ 93 252 84 49 ▪ Closed Mon

An old-style, family-run tapas bar that has been serving fresh seafood tapas to locals for decades.

10 El Vaso de Oro
MAP F5 ▪ C/Balboa 6 ▪ 933 19 30 98

A traditional bar, El Vaso de Oro has served ice-cold beer and fresh tapas for more than half a century. Grab a stool at the long, narrow counter early; it gets packed very quickly.

Restaurants and Cafés

PRICE CATEGORIES

For a three-course meal for one with half a bottle of wine (or equivalent meal), including taxes and extra charges.

€ under €35   €€ €35–50   €€€ over €50

1 Set Portes
MAP N5 ■ Pg Isabel II 14 ■ 93 319 30 33 ■ €€

Founded in 1836, this legendary city institution serves some of the finest Catalan cuisine in the city, including a variety of paellas.

2 El Filferro
MAP F6 ■ C/Sant Carles 29 ■ 600 83 66 74 ■ Open 10–1am Wed–Sun ■ €

This charming café (see p64), with tables set on the square, is perfect for coffee and cake, a delicious light lunch of Mediterranean specialities or a vermut on a summer evening.

3 Green Spot
MAP P5 ■ C/Reina Cristina 12 ■ 93 802 55 65 ■ €€

A spacious restaurant with sleek, minimalist design, Green Spot serves some of the best vegan and vegetarian food in the city.

4 Somorrostro
MAP F6 ■ C/Sant Carles 11 ■ 93 225 00 10 ■ Open 1pm–midnight daily ■ €€

Sample the superb Catalan dishes prepared with fresh ingredients at this chic restaurant. The menu here changes daily, and the decor generates a relaxed, welcoming vibe.

5 Brunch & Cake By The Sea
MAP F5 ■ Pg Joan de Borbó 5 ■ 93 138 35 72 ■ Open 10am–7pm daily ■ €

Furnished with a rustic decor, this bright café features an extensive brunch menu of classics such as eggs Benedict. Find vegan and gluten-free options as well as great cakes.

6 Salamanca
MAP F6 ■ C/Almirall Cervera 34 ■ 93 221 50 33 ■ €€

This may feel like a tourist trap at first, but the food is top notch. There are plenty of meat dishes on offer.

7 La Roseta
MAP F6 ■ C/Meer 37 ■ 673 81 69 76 ■ Open 8:30am–2:30pm daily ■ €

A cosy spot that offers homemade cakes, including a legendary cheese-cake, as well as great coffee.

8 El Gallito
Passeig del Mare Nostrum 19 ■ 933 12 35 85 ■ €€

This stylish spot serves a range of delicacies, including Mediterranean rice seafood dishes.

9 Oaxaca
MAP F5 ■ Pla de Palau 20 ■ 93 319 00 64 ■ Open 1pm–midnight daily ■ €€

One of the best Mexican restaurants in the city, Oaxaca serves creative dishes such as Sopa Azteca con tortillas (soup) or quesadillas with spider crab.

10 La Mar Salada
MAP E6 ■ Pg de Joan de Borbó 58 ■ 93 221 21 27 ■ Open 1–4pm Mon–Tue, 1–4pm and 8–11pm Wed–Fri, 1:30–4pm and 8:30–11pm Sat, 1–4:30pm Sun ■ €€

Light and bright, this restaurant serves modern fare with an emphasis on seafood, such as monkfish served with wild mushrooms and paella.

Tàrtar de sorell at La Mar Salada

See map on pp100–101 ←

🔟 Eixample

If the old town is the heart of Barcelona, and green Tibidabo and Montjuïc its lungs, the Eixample is its nervous system – its economic and commercial core. The area took shape in 1860, when the city was allowed to expand beyond the medieval walls. Based on plans by Catalan engineer Ildefons Cerdà, the Eixample is laid out on a grid. Construction continued into the 20th century at a time when the elite was patronizing the most daring architects. *Modernisme* was flourishing and the area became home to the best of Barcelona's Modernista architecture, with its elegant façades and

Rooftop, La Pedrera

balconies. Today, enchanting cafés, funky design shops, gourmet restaurants and hip bars draw the professional crowd, which has adopted the neighbourhood as its own.

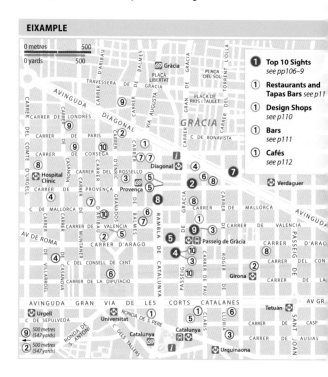

EIXAMPLE

1 **Top 10 Sights** see pp106–9
1 **Restaurants and Tapas Bars** see p11
1 **Design Shops** see p110
1 **Bars** see p111
1 **Cafés** see p112

1 Sagrada Família

Gaudí's wizardry culminated in this enchanting, wild, unconventional church *(see pp12–15)*, which dominates the city skyline.

2 La Pedrera

A daring, surreal fantasyland, and Gaudí's most remarkable civic work *(see pp26–7)*.

3 Sant Pau Recinte Modernista

MAP H1 ■ C/Sant Antoni Maria Claret 167 ■ 93 553 78 11 ■ Opening times vary, check website ■ Adm; guided tours in English 11am daily ■ www.santpaubarcelona.org

Founded in 1401, the Hospital de la Santa Creu i de Sant Pau *(see pp44–5)* was a fully-functioning hospital until 2009, when all medical activities were moved to a new building and the UNESCO World Heritage Site exquisitely restored and opened

Sant Pau Recinte Modernista

to the public as a cultural centre. The Art Nouveau site, created by Domènech i Montaner between 1902 and 1930, is a tribute to *Modernisme* – and Domènech's answer to Gaudí's Sagrada Família. There are eight pavilions, which recall the history of Catalonia using murals, mosaics and sculptures, and other buildings, all linked by underground tunnels. The buildings are interlaced by gardens and courtyards. The site is part of the Ruta del Modernisme *(see p137)*.

4 Mansana de la Discòrdia

MAP E2 ■ Pg de Gràcia 35–45

At the heart of the city's *Quadrat d'Or* (Golden Square) lies this stunning row of houses. The "block of discord" is so named because of the dramatic contrast between its three flagship buildings. Built between 1900 and 1907 by the three Modernista greats, rival architects Gaudí, Domènech i Montaner and Puig i Cadafalch, the houses were commissioned by competing bourgeois families. Domènech is represented by the ornate Casa Lleó Morera *(see p45)*, Puig by the Gothic-inspired Casa Amatller *(see p45)*, and Gaudí by the whimsical Casa Batlló *(see p45)*. Among them, the Casa Amatller and Casa Batlló can be toured. The houses at Nos. 37 and 39 add to the splendour of the block. At No. 39 is the Museu del Perfum *(see p43)*.

ILDEFONS CERDÀ

Ildefons Cerdà's design for the new city, comprising a uniform grid of square blocks, received backing in 1859. Reflecting Cerdà's utopian socialist ideals, each block was to have a garden-like courtyard surrounded by uniform flats. Real estate vultures soon intervened, though, and the courtyards were converted into warehouses and factories. Today these green spaces are gradually being reinstated.

The Els Encants market space

6 Els Encants
MAP H3 ■ Av Meridiana 69
■ Open 9am–8pm Mon, Wed, Fri, Sat
■ https://encantsbarcelona.com

For almost a hundred years, the Els Encants market *(see p68)* was a rambling, chaotic jumble of street stalls. In 2014 it got a striking new home and now its stalls are arranged in a gentle upward spiral under a mirrored canopy designed to keep off the sun. As well as antiques, curiosities and other general bric-a-brac, you'll find textiles, household goods, records and vintage clothes here.

7 Casa Terrades – "Casa de les Punxes"
MAP F2 ■ Av Diagonal 416

This Gothic-style castle with four towers was designed by Modernista architect Josep Puig i Cadafalch and finished in 1905 for the Terrades sisters who owned several buildings on this street. It has always housed private homes, and today it also contains a co-working space. From the outside you can admire the forged ironwork on the balconies, the carved reliefs and the colourful stained-glass windows. The ceramic panels mounted on the façade represent the patriotic symbols of Catalonia.

Cloud and Chair, **Fundació Tàpies**

5 Fundació Tàpies
MAP E2 ■ C/Aragó 255
■ Open 10am–7pm Tue–Thu & Sat (to 3pm Sun) ■ Adm (free for under 16s) ■ https://fundaciotapies.org

Paintings and sculptures by Antoni Tàpies (1923–2012), Catalonia's foremost artist, are housed in this early Modernista building *(see pp32–3)*. For a glimpse of what awaits inside, look up – crowning the museum is the artist's eye-catching wire sculpture *Cloud and Chair* (1990). The collection of over 300 pieces covers Tàpies' whole range of work, including abstract pieces such as *Grey Ochre on Brown* (1962). Temporary exhibitions are also held here, with past shows by Mario Herz and Hans Hacke.

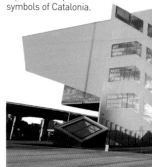

8 Rambla de Catalunya
MAP E2

This elegant extension of the better-known Rambla is a more upmarket version. Lined with trees that form a leafy green tunnel in summer, it features scores of pretty façades and shops, including the Modernista Farmàcia Bolos (No. 77). The avenue (see pp66–7) teems with terrace bars and cafés.

9 Museu Egipci
MAP E2 ■ C/València 284
■ 93 488 01 88 ■ Open 11am–3pm & 4–7:30pm Mon–Sat, 10am–2pm Sun
■ Adm ■ www.museuegipci.com

Spain's most important Egyptology museum houses more than 350 exhibits from over 3,000 years of Ancient Egyptian history. Exhibits include terracotta figures, human and animal mummies, and a bust of the goddess Sekhmet (700–300 BC).

10 Museu del Disseny de Barcelona
MAP H3 ■ Pl de les Glòries Catalanes 37–38 ■ 93 256 68 00 ■ Open 10am–8pm Tue–Sun ■ https://ajuntament. barcelona.cat/museudeldisseny

A monolithic hulk hosts this museum showcasing architecure, fashion, product and graphic design. The glass-and-zinc-clad building is a design statement in its own right. It also houses two leading independent, non-profit associations promoting design and architecture, the Foment de les Arts i del Disseny (FAD) and Barcelona Centre de Disseny (BCD).

Disseny Museum

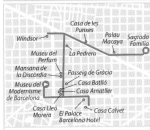

THE MODERNISTA ROUTE

[Map showing: Casa de les Punxes, Palau Macaya, Sagrada Família, Windsor, Museu del Perfum, La Pedrera, Mansana de la Discòrdia, Passeig de Gràcia, Museu del Modernisme de Barcelona, Casa Batlló, Casa Amatller, Casa Lleó Morera, El Palace Barcelona Hotel, Casa Calvet]

▶ MORNING

Visit the **Museu del Modernisme de Barcelona** (C/Balmes 48, www. mmbcn.cat) for an introduction to Catalan Art Nouveau via a series of temporary exhibitions, then stroll around the gardens of the university. Head east along Gran Via past the **El Palace Barcelona Hotel** (see p142) and turn right down C/Bruc and right again onto C/Casp for a glimpse of Gaudí's **Casa Calvet** (see p113). Walk two blocks west to the majestic Pg de Gràcia; then go right again three blocks to the **Mansana de la Discòrdia** (see p107) and explore **Casa Lleó Morera, Casa Amatller** or **Casa Batlló** – or all three (see p45) if you have the time. Sniff around the **Museu del Perfum** and **Regia** perfume shop (see p110) before continuing north to marvel at Gaudí's **La Pedrera** (see pp26–7). Take a lunch break at **Windsor** (see p113). Their set menu is an enjoyable way to experience Catalan haute cuisine.

AFTERNOON

After lunch, return to Pg de Gràcia then turn right along Av Diagonal, taking in the fairytale **Casa de les Punxes** (see p45) at No. 416. Continue on Diagonal, turning left at Pg Sant Joan to see the exhibition on Modernism in the Palau Macaya at No. 108. Then stroll along C/Mallorca to the **Sagrada Família** (see pp12–15). Here you can take in the Nativity Façade and rest weary legs in the Plaça de Gaudí before climbing the bell towers for a breathtaking view of the city.

See map on pp106–7

Design Shops

A dazzling display at Pilma

1 Pilma
MAP E1 ■ Av Diagonal 403
■ Closed Sun ■ www.pilma.com

This shop sells modern furniture and interior accessories by big names, as well as cutting-edge creations by a range of Catalan designers.

2 DomésticoShop
MAP D1 ■ C/ Diagonal 419
■ Closed Sun ■ www.domestico
shop.com

A household name in the interior design world, this split-level shop has furniture, domestic knick-knacks and a cute café.

3 Regia
MAP E2 ■ Pg de Gràcia 39
■ Closed Sun ■ www.regia.es

The biggest perfume shop in the city has over 1,000 scents to choose from, including all the leading brands, and smaller makers. The space also plays host to the Museu del Perfum (see p43).

4 Dos i Una
MAP E2 ■ C/Roselló 275
■ 932 17 70 32

This designer gift shop with a steel-tiled floor and psychedelic colour scheme sells "made in Barcelona" items and souvenirs.

5 Odd Kiosk
MAP D2 ■ C/Valéncia 222

Barcelona's first LGBTQ+ news kiosk is slick and is packed with style magazines, fanzines and cards.

6 Nanimarquina
MAP F2 ■ Rosselló 256
■ Closed Sun & Mon ■ https://
nanimarquina.com

Exquisite handmade carpets and textiles are sold in this artful shop.

7 Azul Tierra
MAP E2 ■ C/Córsega 276–282
■ Closed Sun & Mon ■ https://
azultierra.es

A huge, warehouse-style space with exquisite furniture as well as lighting and all kinds of decorative objects ranging from mirrors to candles.

8 Àmbit
MAP F2 ■ C/Aragó 338
■ 93 459 24 20

This huge showroom has a wide range of furniture from top designers, plus a selection of kilims, carpets, cushions, mirrors and other decorative objects.

The chic and cosy Nordik Think

9 Nordik Think
MAP D1 ■ C/Casanova 214
■ Closed Sun ■ www.en.nordicthink.
com/showroom

This beautiful showroom for Scandinavian design displays elegant and minimalist furnishings, lighting, decorative objects and much more by top designers from northern Europe.

10 Bagués Joieria
MAP E2 ■ Pg de Gràcia 41
■ Closed Sun ■ www.bagues-
masriera.com

Every piece at this jewellery shop is handmade using traditional methods

Bars

1 Milano
MAP E3 ■ Ronda Universitat 35
■ 93 112 71 50 ■ Opening times vary

Sip on your cocktails while lounging on the red-velvet sofas at Milano. There are periodic live jazz performances as well.

2 Xixbar
MAP C4 ■ C/Rocafort 19 ■ 93 416 13 99 ■ Opening times vary

A highly reputed bar that prepares gin and tonics with the city's best spirits sold in the shop next door.

3 Les Gens Que J'aime
MAP E2 ■ C/Valencia 286
■ 93 215 68 79 ■ Open 6pm–2:30am Mon–Thu & Sun, 7pm–3am Fri–Sat

This is an ideal place to have a drink and enjoy lounge music after exploring the area around Passeig de Gràcia and Rambla Catalunya.

4 Slow Bar
MAP D1 ■ C/París 186 ■ 93 368 14 55 ■ Open 7pm–5am Mon–Fri, 6pm–6am Sat (club Fri & Sat only)

This red-hued bar also has a club and live music venue. It offers a range of cocktails which you can sample.

5 Bar Marfil
MAP E2 ■ Rambla de Catalunya 104 ■ 93 550 06 00 ■ Open 8am–midnight daily

Located inside Hotel Murmuri, this is a trendy bar on a fancy shopping street. Sink into a plush faux-Baroque armchair and sip a cocktail.

6 Cotton House Hotel Terrace
MAP F3 ■ Gran Via de les Corts Catalans 670 ■ 93 450 50 45 ■ Open 7am–midnight daily

A jungle of plants, elegant wicker

furnishings and fabulous cocktails make this chic hotel terrace bar *(see p61)* the perfect place for a drink.

7 Ideal
MAP D2 ■ C/Aribau 89 ■ 93 453 10 28 ■ Open noon–2:30am daily

Opened by legendary barman José María Gotarda in 1931, this place offers more than 80 kinds of whisky.

8 Jardin del Alma
MAP E2 ■ C/Mallorca 271
■ 93 216 44 78 ■ Open 5–9pm daily

An enchanting secret garden awaits at this chic hotel *(see p61)*. Sink into a plush sofa and enjoy a glass of wine and some tapas.

9 Ajoblanco
MAP E1 ■ C/Tuset 20 ■ 93 667 87 66 ■ Open 1pm–midnight Mon–Wed (until 3am Thu & Fri), 8pm–3am Sat

This is a hotspot for cocktails, with live music on Wednesdays and DJs on the weekends.

10 Dry Martini
MAP D2 ■ C/Aribau 162 ■ 93 217 50 72 ■ Open 1pm–2:30am Mon–Thu (to 3am Fri), 4:30pm–3am Sat (to 2:30am Sun)

An elegant venue to enjoy cocktails prepared by talented bartenders. Jazz sounds play in the background.

Bar area at Dry Martini

See map on pp106–7

Cafés

Gallery and eating spot Café Cosmo, decorated with artworks

1 Laie Llibreria Cafè
MAP E3 ■ C/Pau Claris 85 ■ 93 318 17 39 ■ Closed Sun

A cultural meeting place with a lively atmosphere, airy terrace and one of the best bookshops in town *(see p64)*. There's an excellent set lunch.

2 Cafè del Centre
MAP F3 ■ C/Girona 69 ■ 93 488 11 01 ■ Closed Mon & Sun

Said to be the oldest café in the Eixample area, with dark wooden interiors that have not changed for a century, this is an unpretentious spot for a quiet coffee.

3 Casa Alfonso
MAP F3 ■ C/Roger de Llúria 6 ■ 93 301 97 83 ■ Closed Sun

This classy café has been in business since 1929. It offers arguably the best *pernil* (serrano ham) in the city.

4 Oma Bistro
MAP D3 ■ C/Consell de Cent 227 ■ 93 348 70 49

A welcoming, loft-style space with colourful, mismatched furnishings, Oma Bistro is a local favourite. It is known for its superb brunch.

5 Pastelerias Mauri
MAP E2 ■ Rambla Catalunya 102 ■ 93 215 10 20 ■ Closed Sun D

One of the best pastry shops in town ever since its opening in 1929. Enjoy a hot drink with an elaborate dessert in Modernista surroundings.

6 Café Cosmo
MAP E2 ■ C/Enric Granados 3 ■ 93 105 79 92

This art gallery café, located on a semi-pedestrianized street, offers sandwiches, cakes and tapas.

7 Baluard
MAP F2 ■ Praktik Bakery Hotel, C/Provença ■ 93 269 48 18 ■ Closed Sun D

Located inside the lobby of a Scandinavian-style urban hotel, this café-bakery offers gourmet salads, sandwiches and pastries.

8 Velódromo
MAP D1 ■ C/Muntaner 213 ■ 93 430 60 22

A historic bar with original 1930s furnishings, Velódromo was reopened by celebrity chef Carles Abellan. The menu features Catalan classics.

9 Manso's Café
MAP C4 ■ C/Manso 1 ■ 93 348 63 46

Enjoy fabulous homemade cakes, great coffee (with a choice of milks), delicious soups and quiches at this café. Eat out on the little terrace or in the cosy interior.

10 Granja Petitbo
MAP D2 ■ C/Mallorca 194 ■ www.granjapetitbo.com

Sink into a sofa and tuck into light meals at this café. Plenty of vegan and vegetarian options are available.

Restaurants and Tapas Bars

PRICE CATEGORIES

For a three-course meal for one with half a bottle of wine (or equivalent meal), including taxes and extra charges.

€ under €35   €€ €35–50   €€€ over €50

1 Joséphine
MAP E2 ■ C/Pau Claris 147
■ 93 853 55 40 ■ €

Coffee and snacks are served all day at this French colonial café. There's also an evening menu.

2 Cinc Sentits
MAP D2 ■ C/Aribau 58 ■ 93 323 94 90 ■ Closed Mon–Wed ■ €€€

Indulge the five senses (cinc sentits in Catalan) at this stylish restaurant where the chef's contemporary interpretations of classic Catalan cuisine have won it two Michelin stars.

3 Igueldo
MAP E2 ■ C/Rosselló 186
■ 93 452 25 55 ■ Closed Sun ■ €€

Updated Basque cuisine is served in elegant surroundings here (see p62).

4 Disfrutar
MAP D2 ■ Carrer de Villarroel, 163 ■ 93 348 68 96 ■ Closed Mon & Sun ■ €€€

Located in front of Ninot market, Disfrutar (see p63) lets you feast on avant-garde dishes that offer a complete gastronomic experience.

5 Casa Carmen
MAP C3 ■ C/Casp 17 ■ 93 412 57 97 ■ Open 12:30–4pm & 7–11:30pm daily ■ €€

This is part of a small chain that combines elegant décor with traditional Spanish cuisine at affordable prices.

6 Cervecería Catalana
MAP E2 ■ C/Mallorca 236
■ 93 216 03 68 ■ €

Some of the best tapas in town served with a variety of beers, close to the Rambla de Catalunya.

7 Windsor
MAP E1 ■ C/Còrsega 286
■ 93 237 75 88 ■ Closed 3 weeks in Aug ■ €€€

Catalan *haute cuisine* is served (see p62) in elegant surroundings with chandeliers and red upholstered furniture. There's also a garden for alfresco dining.

8 La Taverna del Clínic
MAP D2 ■ C/Rosselló 155
■ 93 410 42 21 ■ Closed Sun ■ €€

This bar (see p62) looks ordinary, but its excellent, contemporary tapas is among the best in the city.

9 Paco Meralgo
MAP D1 ■ C/Muntaner 171
■ 93 430 90 27 ■ €

A bright, stylish tapas bar, Paco Meralgo has a gourmet menu based on recipes from around the country.

10 Moments
MAP E3 ■ Pg de Gràcia 38–40
■ 93 151 87 81 ■ Closed Tue–Thu L & Sun ■ €€€

Set in the ultra-luxurious Mandarin Oriental (see p145), Moments has been awarded two Michelin stars for its sublime renditions of Catalan classics, from langoustine tartare to scallops with artichokes. A la carte and tasting menus offered.

Moments at the Mandarin Oriental

See map on pp106–7

🔟 Gràcia, Tibidabo and Zona Alta

The hilly Zona Alta covers several neighbourhoods, from the moneyed Pedralbes and Tibidabo to bohemian Gràcia. The area offers stunning views and regal attractions, but what sets it apart are its 15 parks – the best are Collserola, spread like green baize over Tibidabo mountain, and Gaudí's Park Güell. Cosmopolitan Gràcia's political tradition and Roma community have long drawn artists and writers to its labyrinthine streets, and its squares are now home to lively bars and stores.

Torre de Collserola

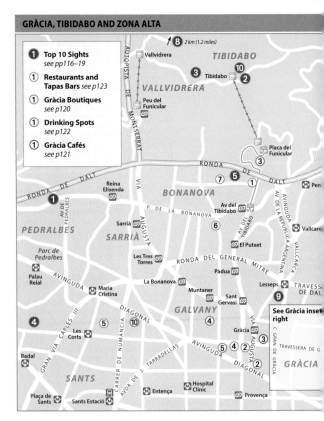

GRÀCIA, TIBIDABO AND ZONA ALTA

1 Top 10 Sights *see pp116–19*

1 Restaurants and Tapas Bars *see p123*

1 Gràcia Boutiques *see p120*

1 Drinking Spots *see p122*

1 Gràcia Cafés *see p121*

Previous pages The surreal façade of the Teatre-Museu Dalí, Figueres

① Monestir de Pedralbes

MAP A1 ■ C/Baixada del Monestir 9 ■ Open Apr–Sep: 10am–5pm Tue–Fri (to 7pm Sat, to 8pm Sun); Oct–Mar: 10am–2pm Tue–Fri (to 5pm Sat & Sun) ■ Adm; free first Sun of the month, every Sun 3–8pm) ■ https://monestir pedralbes.barcelona

Named after the Latin *petras albas*, which means "white stones", this outstandingly beautiful Gothic monastery *(see p40)* was founded by Queen Elisenda de Montcada de Piños in 1327 with the support of her husband James II of Aragón. Her alabaster tomb lies in the wall between the church and the impressive three-storey Gothic cloister. The furnished kitchens, cells, infirmary

The Gothic Monestir de Pedralbes

and refectory, which are all well preserved, provide an interesting glimpse into medieval life.

② Parc d'Atraccions del Tibidabo

MAP B1 ■ Pl de Tibidabo ■ Opening times vary, check website ■ Adm ■ www.tibidabo.cat

Take the funicular up to the top of Tibidabo's 517-m (1,695-ft) mountain to visit this traditional amusement park, which opened in 1908 *(see p52)*. There are a couple of white-knuckle rides, but the real attractions are the old-fashioned ones, including a beautifully preserved carousel and a Ferris wheel. There's also the Museu dels Autòmates *(see p43)*, with automatons, mechanical models and a scale model of the park.

③ Torre de Collserola

MAP B1 ■ Parc de Collserola ■ Opening times vary, check website ■ Adm ■ www.torrede collserola.com

This slender telecommunications tower was designed by British architect Sir Norman Foster. The needle-like upper structure rests on a concrete pillar, anchored by 12 huge steel cables. Rising to a height of 288 m (945 ft), the top is reached by a glass-fronted lift. On a clear day, you can see Montserrat and the Pyrenees.

The grand Camp Nou, FC Barcelona's home stadium

FC Barcelona Museum and Stadium Tour

MAP A2 ■ Entrance 9 Stadium, Av Arístides Maillol ■ Opening times vary, check website; advance booking recommended ■ Adm ■ www.fc barcelona.com

The Museu del FC Barcelona (see p42), Barcelona's most visited museum, is a must for the fans. Numerous displays of football memorabilia show all you need to know about the club. Work donated by some of Catalonia's top artists is also on display. Admission includes access to Barca's 100,000-seater stadium, Camp Nou, a monument to the city's love affair with the game.

CosmoCaixa Museu de la Ciència

MAP B1 ■ C/Isaac Newton 26 ■ 93 212 60 50 ■ Open 10am–8pm daily ■ Adm (free for under 16s) ■ https://cosmo caixa.org/es/museo-ciencia-barcelona

Barcelona's science museum is a thoroughly stimulating and interactive affair. It occupies a glass-and-steel building, with six of its nine storeys set underground. Displays include a wide range of historic objects, flora and fauna. One of its most important pieces is a recreated section of flooded Amazon rainforest, including fish, reptiles, mammals, birds and plants. A tour through Earth's geological history explains processes such as erosion and sedimentation. There are also innovative temporary exhibitions on environmental issues (see p43).

Park Güell

A UNESCO World Heritage Site, this heady brew of architectural wizardry (see pp22–3) includes *trencadís* tiling, fairy-tale pavilions, Gothic archways and the columned Sala Hipóstila (originally designed as a market hall). In true Gaudí style, playfulness and symbolism pervade every aspect of the park. The Casa-Museu Gaudí, where Gaudí lived for 20 years, is dedicated to his life.

⑦ Parc del Laberint d'Horta

MAP C1 ■ C/German Desvalls ■ Open 10am–dusk daily ■ Adm; free Wed, Sun

In 1802, the Marquès d'Alfarràs hosted a huge party in these wonderful Neo-Classical gardens in honor of Charles IV. Designed by Italian architect Domenico Bagutti, they feature pavilions, a lake, a waterfall, canals and a cypress-tree hedge maze. The gardens are closed in November.

GRÀCIA

Until the late 19th century, Gràcia was a fiercely proud independent city. Despite locals' protests, it became part of Barcelona proper in 1898, but has maintained a sense of separatism and has been a hotbed of political activity. It is now home to a booming cottage industry nurtured by a growing band of artisans. Do not miss the *barri's* annual fiesta (see p72) in the second week of August.

8 Parc de Collserola

MAP B1 ▪ Info point:
C/Església 92 ▪ 93 280 35 52
▪ https://parcnaturalcollserola.cat

Beyond the peaks of Tibidabo mountain, this 6,500-ha (16,000-acre) natural park of wild forest and winding paths is an oasis of calm. It is great for hiking and biking, with signposted paths and nature trails.

9 Casa Vicens

Carrer de les Carolines 20
▪ Open Apr–Oct: 10am–8pm daily;
Nov–Mar: 10am–3pm Mon (to 7pm Tue–Sun) ▪ Adm ▪ www.casavicens.org

Gaudí's first major commission, this former private home (see p45) is situated on a quiet residential street. It was once surrounded by orchards and fields, a fact the architect has referenced on the façade; a patchwork of tiles decorated with marigolds. Inside, rooms are replete with florid marquetry, arabesque detailing and nature-inspired ambiances.

10 Temple Expiatori del Sagrat Cor

The Neo-Gothic Temple of the Sacred Heart (see p40) was built by Enric Sagnier between 1902 and 1911. It has a dramatic sculpture of Jesus, and an elaborate door. Take the elevator up the main tower, or climb up to the outside terrace for great views.

Temple Expiatori del Sagrat Cor

EXPLORING THE HEIGHTS

▶ **MORNING**

Taking the northern route of the Bus Turístic is the easiest way to negotiate the vast northern area of Barcelona; it also gives discounts on entrance to major sights en route. Start off at **Plaça de Catalunya** (see p46) – tickets can be bought on board – and sit on the top deck for a good view of the Modernista magic along Pg de Gràcia. Make the whimsical **Park Güell** your first stop and spend the morning ambling around Gaudí's otherworldly park. Get back on the bus and continue north to the southern end of Av Tibidabo. Walk about 500 m (1,600 ft) up Av Tibidabo and stop off for a leisurely lunch in the garden of the palatial **El Asador d'Aranda** (see p123).

AFTERNOON

After you've had your fill of fine Castilian cuisine, stroll up Av Tibidabo to Plaça Doctor Andreu, where you can hop on the funicular train to go higher still to Plaça de Tibidabo. Pop into the **Parc d'Atraccions** (see p117) for a ride on the dodgems or the Ferris wheel. Then head over to the landmark **Torre de Collserola** (see p117), where a glass elevator whisks you up to an observation deck for spectacular views. Return to Pl Doctor Andreu on the funicular and treat yourself to a granissat (see p65) in one of the terrace bars. Catch the number 196 bus down the Av Tibidabo, then take Bus Turístic back to the city centre.

Gràcia Boutiques

Contemporary fashion at Boo

1 Boo
C/Bonavista 2 ▪ 93 368 14 58 ▪ Open 11am–8:30pm Mon–Sat

An elegantly decorated space, Boo offers contemporary men's clothing and accessories with a vintage feel. International labels like Saint James, Norse Projects and tailored shirts by Tuk Tuk are available. There's also a selection of books and colognes.

2 Lydia Delgado
C/Séneca 28 ▪ 93 218 16 30 ▪ Open noon–8pm Mon–Fri, 11am–2pm Sat

This well-established Catalan designer creates clothing for women inspired by the 1950s and 1960s. Touches of embroidery, patchwork and other details enliven the fabrics.

3 José Rivero
C/Astúries 43 ▪ 93 237 33 88 ▪ Open 11am–2pm & 5–9pm Mon–Sat

José provides his own original in-house creations for men and women; he also sells accessories by young, local designers.

4 Berta Sumpsi
MAP F1 ▪ C/Verdi 98 ▪ 676 870 122 ▪ Open 11am–2pm & 5–8pm Mon–Sat

This space doubles as a workshop and showroom. There is a wide range of simple, sculptural jewellery displayed in minimal surroundings.

5 Érase Una Vez
C/Bonavista 13 ▪ 697 805 409 ▪ Open 10:30am–2pm & 5–8pm Mon–Fri, 11am–2pm Sat

Literally translating to "once upon a time", this shop creates unique wedding gowns. It also stocks some of the most exclusive designers.

6 The Vos Shop
C/ Verdi 24 ▪ 93 311 21 14 ▪ Open 11am–9pm Mon–Sat

The vibe of Gràcia is captured in this boutique that stocks creations of young, local designers. Collections range from bright overalls to graphic t-shirts for men and women.

7 Velvet BCN
MAP F1 ▪ C/Verdi 42 ▪ 93 126 94 73 ▪ www.velvetbcn.com

One of several chic little boutiques on C/Verdi, Velvet BCN sells beautiful women's clothing and accessories, all made sustainably.

8 Mushi Mushi
C/Bonavista 12 ▪ 93 292 29 74 ▪ Open 11am–2:30pm & 4:30–8:30pm Mon–Sat

From hard-to-find small labels to the best international collections, Mushi Mushi stocks a selection of women's fashion and accessories.

9 El Piano
C/Verdi 20 bis ▪ 93 415 51 76 ▪ Open 11am–2:30pm & 4:30–8:30pm Mon–Fri, 11am–9pm Sat

El Piano sells elegant and stylish womenswear with a retro flair made by Catalan designer Tina García. It also stocks clothes by other independent designers.

10 Botó and Co
C/Bonavista 3 ▪ 93 676 22 71 ▪ Open 10am–9pm Mon–Sat

This multibrand store sells high-quality women's fashion, including Current/Elliot jeans, Humanoid sweaters, and more.

Gràcia Cafés

1 Cafè del Sol
MAP F1 ■ Pl del Sol 16
■ 93 237 14 48

This café-bar is a cut above the others in the lively Plaça del Sol. The atmosphere buzzes, the conversation inspires and the excellent coffee keeps on coming.

2 Cafè Salambó
MAP F1 ■ C/Torrijos 51
■ 93 218 69 66

Scrumptious sandwiches and salads are the draw at this bar and café. There are pool tables upstairs.

3 Bar Quimet
MAP E1 ■ C/Vic 23
■ 93 218 41 89

An old-fashioned bar with marble-topped tables and big wooden barrels, this is a great spot for an aperitif. Try the *vermut* (vermouth) and a selection of olives and *boquerones* (fresh anchovies).

4 La Cafetera
MAP F1 ■ Pl de la Virreina 2
■ 93 667 79 38

Of all the cafés on Plaça de la Virreina, La Cafetera, with its outdoor terrace and tiny patio full of potted plants, is perhaps one of the nicest options for a quiet and leisurely morning coffee and a sandwich or pastry.

Alfresco dining at La Cafetera

5 Suís & Bowls
Travessera de Gràcia 151
■ 93 415 3698

This colourful café serves healthy meals and fresh salads. Additionally, fresh juices, cakes and pastries are also on offer.

6 Mama's Café
MAP F1 ■ C/Torrijos 26
■ 93 210 00 50 ■ Closed Tue

A pretty minimalist spot with a small patio at the back. Organic sandwiches, salads and homemade cakes are served all day, as well as fresh fruit juices and cocktails.

7 Bicioci Bike Café
MAP F1 ■ C/Venus 1
■ 93 458 20 44

Bikes hang from the ceiling at this café. Here you will also find excellent coffee, homemade cakes, brunches and daily lunch specials.

8 Cafè del Teatre
MAP F1 ■ C/Torrijos 41
■ 93 416 06 51

This is a great place to find a young, friendly crowd and good conversation. The only connection with the theatre, however, seems to be the velvet curtains on the sign over the door of this scruffy yet popular café.

9 La Nena
MAP F1 ■ C/Ramón y Cajal 36
■ 93 285 14 76

The room with tables and games for children here makes this a popular choice with parents of young kids. The range of homemade cakes, juices and hot drinks on offer are a neighbourhood favourite.

10 Sabio Infante
MAP F1 ■ C/Torrent de l'Olla 39 ■ 93 720 46 36 ■ Closed Mon

Homemade cakes and great coffee are the draw at Sabio Infante, which is decorated with all sorts of weird and wonderful kitsch finds.

See map on pp116–17

Drinking Spots

The bar area at Bobby Gin

1 Bobby Gin
MAP E1 ■ C/Francisco Giner 47
■ www.bobbygin.com

This cocktail bar stocks some 60 premium gins – floral, citric, spiced and vintage. Their slogan, "Respect the gin", comes courtesy of the eponymous bartender.

2 Las Vermudas
MAP F1 ■ C/Robíe 32 ■ Closed Mon ■ www.lasvermudas.com/en/home_en

Vermut (vermouth) shows no signs of losing popularity, and Las Vermudas features a fantastic selection of it. Enjoy a glass out on the terrace, or at one of the live concerts.

3 Mirablau
Pl Dr Andreu ■ Closed Thu
■ http://mirablaubcn.cat

A slightly older, well-heeled set who adhere to the smart dress code come to this bar for a combination of cocktails and views of the city.

4 Gimlet
C/Santaló 46 ■ Closed Sun
■ www.drymartiniorg.com

Opened in 1982 by Javier de las Muelas, a well-known name on the international cocktail scene, Gimlet is a classic bar with contemporary flair, where you can enjoy premium drinks in elegant surroundings.

5 Luz de Gas
MAP D1 ■ C/Muntaner 246
■ Closed Sun–Tue ■ www.luzdegas.com

A major player since the mid-1990s, this former theatre retains plenty of its retro charm with red velvet drapes and chandeliers. It now features live bands and DJs.

6 El Tresss Bar
MAP F1 ■ C/Alzina 2

Tucked away behind the Plaça de la Virreina, this friendly spot is furnished with quirky vintage finds. It has a cosy atmosphere and a pretty terrace – ideal for relaxing.

7 Torre Rosa
C/Francesc Tàrrega 22
■ Closed L daily ■ www.torrerosa.com

This neighbourhood favourite *(see p61)* is ideal for escaping the summer heat, with tables scattered under a cluster of palm trees. There is a wide range of cocktails on offer.

8 La Cervesera Artesana
MAP F1 ■ C/Sant Agustí 14

A friendly microbrewery, this spot serves a good range of imported beers in addition to their own excellent brews. The Iberian Pale Ale, a mellow amber beer, is certainly worth a try.

9 Elephanta
Torrent d'en Vidalet, 37
■ www.elephanta.cat

Specializing in choicest flavoured gins, Elephanta also offers perfectly mixed cocktails, served in a cheerful intimate space. The bar doubles as a mellow cafe during early evenings.

10 Bikini
Av Diagonal 547 ■ Closed Mon & Tue ■ Adm ■ www.bikinibcn.com

Open from midnight, this huge venue has three spaces, offering dance and Latin music and a cocktail lounge. Regular live music includes some of the best acts in Europe.

Restaurants and Tapas Bars

1 El Asador d'Aranda
Av Tibidabo 31 ▪ 93 417 01 15 ▪ €€

Set in the magnificent Modernista Casa Roviralta, this restaurant (see p62) is a magnet for businesspeople. Order the delicious lamb roasted in an oak-burning oven and dine in the beautiful garden.

2 Hofmann
MAP E1 ▪ C/La Granada del Penedès 14–16 ▪ 93 218 71 65 ▪ Closed Sat L, Sun, Easter Week, Aug, Christmas ▪ €€€

Established by the late chef Mey Hofmann, this Michelin-starred spot serves exceptional Catalan cuisine. Save room for the desserts.

3 Abissínia
MAP F1 ▪ C/Torrent de les Flors 55 ▪ 93 213 07 85 ▪ Closed Tue ▪ €

Tasty Ethiopian stews are served with *injera* bread here. This is a good restaurant for vegetarians.

4 Il Giardinetto
MAP E1 ▪ C/La Granada del Penedès 28 ▪ 93 218 75 36 ▪ Closed Tue ▪ €€

This restaurant features whimsical, garden-themed decor and serves classic Mediterranean dishes with a twist such as spaghetti alla Sofia Loren (pasta served with anchovy and parsley sauce).

5 Fragments Café
Pl de la Concòrdia 12 ▪ 93 419 96 13 ▪ Closed Mon ▪ €

Plaça de la Concòrdia, in the Les Corts neighbourhood, retains a small-town appeal. Gourmet tapas and cocktails are served in the lovely garden (see p61) at the back.

6 Bonanova
C/Sant Gervasi de Cassoles 103 ▪ 93 417 10 33 ▪ Closed Sun D, Mon ▪ €€

Away from the tourist routes, Bonanova has been serving fresh, seasonal fare cooked in a simple and traditional way since 1964.

7 La Balsa
C/Infanta Isabel 4 ▪ 93 211 50 48 ▪ Closed Tue, Wed & Sun D, Mon, Easter, Aug L ▪ €€

With two garden terraces, La Balsa is a beautiful spot in the Bonanova area, serving fine Basque, Catalan and Mediterranean dishes.

8 Pappa e Citti
MAP F1 ▪ C/Encarnació 38 ▪ 687 657 111 ▪ Closed Sun ▪ €

A cosy restaurant, this place offers wonderful Sardinian dishes. Try the platter of breads, cheeses, cured meats or the stews or pastas.

9 Bar Vall
MAP F1 ▪ Plaça Rovira i Trias ▪ 93 213 34 24 ▪ €

Traditional and friendly bar set in one of Gràcia's prettiest squares serving sandwiches, salads and tapas, as well as more substantial meals.

10 Botafumeiro
MAP E1 ▪ C/Gran de Gràcia 81 ▪ 93 218 42 30 ▪ €€€

The fish tanks here teem with crabs and lobsters destined for dinner plates. Try the *pulpo Gallego* (Galician octopus). Be sure to book ahead.

Exterior of Botafumeiro

See map on pp116–17

TOP 10 Beyond Barcelona

Teatre-Museu Dalí

Steeped in tradition, with its own language and pride in its identity, Catalonia is rich in both cultural heritage and physical beauty. It is not hyperbole to say that Catalonia has everything. The coastline has beautiful sandy beaches, intimate rocky coves and clear waters, while to the north are the 3,000-m (9,840-ft) Pyrenean peaks. These natural treasures are complemented by fabulous churches and monasteries in stunning mountain settings. The cuisine is rewarding, while the local *cava* holds its own against its French champagne counterparts.

BEYOND BARCELONA

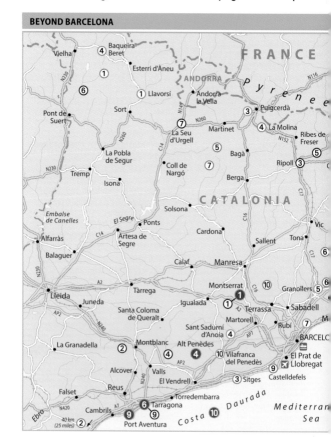

1 Montserrat

Tourist Information: Pl de la Creu; 93 877 77 01 ■ **www. montserratvisita.com**

The dramatic Montserrat mountain, with its remote Benedictine monastery (dating from 1025), is a religious symbol and a place of pilgrimage for the Catalan people. The basilica houses a statue of the patron saint of Catalonia, La Moreneta, also known as the "Black Virgin" *(see p41)*. Some legends date the statue to AD 50, but research suggests it was carved in the 12th century. The monastery was largely destroyed in 1811, during the War of Independence, and rebuilt some 30 years later.

The monastery at Montserrat

Montserrat – Catalan for "jagged mountain" – forms part of a ridge that rises suddenly from the plains. Take the funicular up to the peaks, where paths run alongside spectacular gorges to numerous hermitages.

2 Teatre-Museu Dalí, Figueres

Teatre-Museu Dalí: Pl Gala-Salvador Dalí, Figueres: 97 267 75 00; opening times vary ■ **Casa-Museu Salvador Dalí: Portlligat, Cadaqués: 97 225 10 15; opening times vary** ■ **Adm** ■ **www.salvador-dali.org**

Salvador Dalí was born in the town of Figueres in 1904. Paying tribute to the artist is the fantastic Teatre-Museu Dalí, which is filled with his eccentric works. Housed in a former theatre, the country's second-most-visited museum (after the Prado in Madrid) provides a unique insight into the artist's extraordinary creations, from *La Cesta de Pan* (1926) to *El Torero Alucinógeno* (1970). A 30-minute drive away, close to the beach town of Cadaqués, the Dalí connection continues. Here, you can visit the Casa-Museu Salvador Dalí, which served as the artist's summer home for nearly 60 years until his death in 1989. These two sights are the main attractions of the 'Dalí triangle'. The third sight that completes this so-called triangle is the Gala Dalí Castle House-Museum located in Púbol, which was his gift to his wife, Gala.

1 Top 10 Sights *see pp124–7*	
1 Places to Eat *see p131*	
1 Outdoor Activities *see p130*	
1 National Parks and Nature Reserves *see p129*	
1 Churches and Monasteries *see p128*	

③ Costa Brava

The Costa Brava is a beautiful stretch of Mediterranean coastline, which runs from Blanes (about 60 km (37 miles) north of Barcelona) all the way to the French border. There are a few big resorts, including Lloret de Mar and Roses, but many of the towns and resorts here, such as Calella de Palfrugell and Tamariu, have remained refreshingly low-key. Cultural highlights include the medieval citadel that crowns Tossa de Mar, and the Thyssen Museum in Sant Feliu de Guíxols. The area also has some excellent seafront hiking paths, the Camins de Ronda.

④ Alt Penedès

Tourist Information: C/Hermengild Ciascar 2, Vilafranca del Penedès; 93 818 12 54 ■ Contact the tourist office for details on all winery visits in the region ■ https://turismevilafranca.com

Catalonia's most famous wine region is the *cava*-producing area of the Penedès. The *cava* brands of Cordoníu and Freixenet have become household names worldwide. Many of the area's wineries and bodegas are open to the public. Cordoníu's is one of the most spectacular, housed in a Modernista building designed by Puig i Cadafalch, with a phenomenal 26 km (16 miles) of cellars on five floors.

⑤ Begur and around

Tourist Information: Av Onze de Setembre 5; 97 262 45 20 ■ https://visitbegur.cat

The elegant hilltop town of Begur, with its ruined 14th-century castle, looks down over pristine wetlands and some of the prettiest coves on the Costa Brava. The town's population quadruples in summer as visitors make this their base for exploring nearby beaches and small, isolated coves. Many of the area's beaches stage jazz concerts during the summer. This is perhaps the best stretch of coastline in Catalonia.

Ruins of Tarragona's Roman wall

⑥ Tarragona

Tourist Information: C/Major 39; 97 725 07 95 ■ www.tarragona turisme.cat

The city of Tarragona was once the capital of Roman Catalonia, and the city's main attractions are from this era. Various archaeological treasures include an impressive amphitheatre and well-preserved Roman walls that lead past the Museu Nacional Arqueològic and the Torre de Pilatos, where Christians were supposedly imprisoned before being thrown to the lions. The Catedral de Santa Tecla *(see p128)* is also in Tarragona.

⑦ Girona

Tourist Information: Rambla de la Llibertat 1; 972 01 00 01 ■ www.girona.cat/turisme

Girona is a beautiful town surrounded by lush green hills. Hidden away in the old town, the atmospheric Jewish quarter, known as El Call, is one of Europe's best-preserved medieval enclaves. Visiting Girona's cathedral *(see p128)* is a must.

Statue, El Call

8 Empúries

C/Puig i Cadafalch s/n,
Empúries ■ 97 277 02 08 ■ Open
10am–5pm (Jun–Sep: to 8pm, Oct–
mid-Nov & mid-Feb–May: to 6pm)
■ Adm; free last Tue of month Oct–
Jun ■ www.macempuries.cat

After Tarragona, Empúries is
Catalonia's second most important
Roman site. Located by the sea, it is
more than 40 ha (99 acres) of land
scattered with Greek and Roman
ruins, the highlights of which are the
remains of a market street, various
temples and a Roman amphitheatre.
It's an ideal spot for those looking to
mix a bit of history with a dip in the sea.

9 PortAventura World

Av Pere Molas, Vila-seca,
Tarragona ■ 97 712 90 57 ■ Opening
times vary, check website ■ Adm
■ www.portaventuraworld.com

This theme park is divided into six
areas, including the Far West and
Polynesia, and has some of Europe's
biggest rollercoasters, as well as
a thrilling Ferrari Land.

10 Costa Daurada and Sitges

Tourist Information: Pl Eduard
Maristany 2, Sitges; 93 894 42 51
■ www.visitsitges.com

With its sandy beaches and shallow
waters, the Costa Daurada is a prime
attraction. Torredembarra is a family
resort, but the crown jewel is Sitges,
the summer home to Barcelona's
chic crowd, and a popular destination
for LGBTQ+ travellers. Restaurants
and bars line Sitges's main boulevard, the Passeig Marítim, while
Modernista architecture is scattered
among the 1970s blocks.

Sitges, as seen from the beach

A SCENIC DRIVE

From Barcelona 85 km (53 miles)

▶ MORNING

This drive should take about
5 hours for the round trip. From
Barcelona take the AP7 motorway
until exit 4, then take the C260
to **Cadaqués**. Just before drop-
ping down to the town, stop at
the viewpoint and take in the
azure coastline and the whitewashed houses of this former
fishing village. Once in Cadaqués,
now one of Catalonia's trendiest
beach towns, wander the charming boutique-filled streets. After
a splash in the sea and a coffee
at one of the chic terrace cafés,
take the road leaving Port Lligat
and head for the lighthouse in
Cap de Creus *(see p129)*. Drive
through the desolately beautiful
landscape of this rocky headland
before doubling back and heading
off to Port de la Selva. The road
twists and winds interminably,
but the picture-perfect scenery
will leave you speechless.

AFTERNOON

Enjoy a seafood lunch at Ca
l'Herminda *(C/Illa 7)*, in the small,
mountain-enclosed Port de la
Selva. Then drive to the neighbouring village of Selva del Mar,
with its tiny river, for a post-
prandial coffee on the terrace
of the Bar Stop *(C/Port de la Selva
1)*, before continuing up to the
Monestir de Sant Pere de Rodes
(see p128). You'll be tempted to
stop frequently on the way up
to take in the views. Don't, because
the best is to be had from the
monastery itself – a sweeping
vista of the whole area. There are
plenty of well-signposted walks
around the mountain top, and it
is worth sticking around to see
the sun set slowly over the bay.

See map on pp124–5 ←

Churches and Monasteries

1 Monestir de Montserrat

Montserrat ■ 93 877 77 01
■ Adm (museums) ■ www.abadia
montserrat.cat

Catalonia's holiest place and its
most visited monastery (see p125)
has beautiful Romanesque art and
a statue of the "Black Virgin".

2 Monestir de Poblet

Off N240, 10 km W of
Montblanc ■ Adm ■ www.poblet.cat

This beautiful working monastery
contains the Gothic Capella de Sant
Jordi, a Romanesque church, and
the Porta Daurada, a doorway that
was gilded for Felipe II's visit in 1564.

3 Monestir de Ripoll

Ripoll ■ 97 270 42 03
■ Adm ■ www.monestirderipoll.cat

The west portal of this monastery
(AD 879) has reputedly the finest
Romanesque carvings in Spain.
Of the original buildings, only the
doorway and cloister remain.

4 Monestir de Santes Creus

Santes Creus, 25 km NW of Montblanc
■ Closed Mon ■ Adm ■ https://patri
moni.gencat.cat/en/monuments

The cloister here (1150) is notable
for the beautifully sculpted capitals
by English artist Reinard Funoll.

5 Sant Joan de les Abadesses

Sant Joan de les Abadesses
■ 97 272 05 99 ■ Adm ■ www.
santjoandelesabadesses.cat

This monastery, established in the
9th century, houses a magnificent
Romanesque sculpture representing
the Descent from the Cross.

6 Sant Climent i Santa Maria de Taüll

138 km N of Lleida ■ 97 369 67 15
■ www.centreromanic.com

These two Romanesque churches,
dating from 1123, are perfect
examples of those that pepper
the Pyrenees. The frescoes are
reproductions of the originals,
now housed in Barcelona's
MNAC (see pp20–21).

7 Catedral de La Seu d'Urgell

La Seu d'Urgell ■ 97 335 32 42 ■ Adm
■ www.laseumedieval.com/en

Dating from around 1040, this
cathedral is one of the most
elegant in Catalonia.

8 Catedral de Girona

Plaça de la Catedral s/n, Girona
■ 97 242 71 89 ■ Adm; Mass free
■ www.catedraldegirona.cat

This cathedral possesses the widest
Gothic nave in Europe, after the
basilica in the Vatican.

9 Catedral de Santa Tecla

Old Town, Tarragona ■ Adm;
Mass free ■ Guided tours ■ www.
tarragonaturisme.cat

At 104 m (340 ft) long, Tarragona's
cathedral is the largest in the region.
Begun in the 12th century, it has an
enchanting cloister.

10 Monestir de Sant Pere de Rodes

22 km E of Figueres ■ Closed Mon
■ Adm ■ https://patrimoni.gencat.
cat/en/monuments

Perched on a hilltop, this medieval
UNESCO World Heritage Site offers
breathtaking views over Cap de
Creus and Port de la Selva.

Monestir de Sant Pere de Rodes

National Parks and Nature Reserves

1 **Parc Nacional d'Aigüestortes i Estany de Sant Maurici**

148 km N of Lleida ▪ https:// parcsnaturals.gencat.cat/ca/ xarxa-de-parcs

The magnificent peaks of Catalonia's only national park are accessible from the village of Espot. You'll discover beautiful waterfalls, lakes and glacial tarns 2,000 m (6,560 ft) up.

2 **Delta de l'Ebre**

28 km SE of Tortosa

A patchwork of paddy fields, the wide expanse of the River Ebre is a nature reserve for migratory birds and has many bird-watching stations.

3 **Parc Natural de la Zona Volcànica de la Garrotxa**

40 km NW of Girona

La Garrotxa last erupted 10,000 years ago. The largest crater is the Santa Margalida, 500 m (1,640 ft) wide. It is best to visit in spring.

4 **Cap de Creus**

36 km E of Figueres

The Pyrenees mountains form Catalonia's most easterly point offering great views of the coastline.

5 **Parc Natural del Cadí-Moixeró**

20 km E of La Seu d'Urgell

Covered in a carpet of conifers and oaks, this mountain range has lush vegetation. Several of the peaks here are over 2,000 m (6,560 ft) high.

6 **Parc Natural del Montseny**

48 km NW of Barcelona ▪ https:// parcs.diba.cat/es/web/montseny

Catalonia's most accessible natural park, these woodland hills are suitable for walkers and mountain bikers, with a vast network of trails. Take the popular climb up Turó de l'Home, the highest peak.

7 **Massís de Pedraforca**

64 km N of Manresa ▪ https://parcsnaturals.gen cat.cat/ca/xarxa-de-parcs

A nature reserve surrounds this outcrop of mountains, a favourite of rock climbers.

8 **Serra de l'Albera**

15 km N of Figueres

The Albera Massif is home to ancient dol-mens, Romanesque sanctuaries and one of the last colonies of the Mediterranean tortoise.

Purple heron, Delta de l'Ebre

9 **Parc Natural dels Aiguamolls de l'Empordà**

15 km E of Figueres

This nature reserve hides a number of birdwatching towers. Those in the Laguna de Vilalt and La Bassa de Gall Mari allow the observation of herons, moorhens and other bird species nesting in spring.

10 **Parc Natural de Sant Llorenç del Munt**

12 km E of Manresa ▪ https://parcs. diba.cat/web/santllorenc

Close to Barcelona, this park is home to large numbers of wild boar. Visit the Romanesque monastery at Cerro de la Mola, which is now a restaurant.

See map on pp124–5

Outdoor Activities

Rafting on La Noguera Pallaresa

① Rafting and Kayaking
Noguera Aventura: Lleida; 97 329 01 76; www.noguera ventura.com

One of Europe's best rivers for whitewater sports is La Noguera Pallaresa in the Pyrenees. Late spring is the best time to go, as the mountain snow begins to thaw.

② Scuba Diving
Aquàtica: L'Estartit; 97 275 06 56; www.aquatica-sub.com

The Reserva Natural de les Illes Medes has thousands of species of fish and red coral reefs. Glass-bottom boats cater to non-divers.

③ Water Sports and Sailing
Club de Mar Sitges: Pg Marítim, Sitges; 93 894 09 05; https://club marsitges.com

Good sailing can be found in Sitges, along with yachts for rent and classes for novices. Canoeing and windsurfing are also available.

④ Skiing
La Molina: 25 km S of Puigcerdà; 97 289 20 31; www.lamolina.cat
■ Baqueira-Beret: 97 363 90 00; www.baqueira.es

La Molina is the most accessible Pyrenean ski-resort from Barcelona, but Baqueira-Beret is where the jet-set goes. Both offer all levels of skiing (including off-piste) from December onwards.

⑤ Golf
Santa Cristina d'Aro: 97 283 70 55 ■ Platja d'Aro: 97 281 67 27

The Costa Brava is one of Europe's top golf destinations; the best courses are around Platja d'Aro.

⑥ Horse Riding
Hípica Can Tramp: Ctra Cànoves; 93 871 16 08; www. hipicacantramp.es

Montseny Natural Park *(see p129)* is ideal for horse riding, with a number of stables.

⑦ Ballooning
Vol de Coloms: 97 268 02 55, 689 47 18 72; www.voldecoloms.cat

A balloon journey over the volcanic area of La Garrotxa is an unbeatable way to get a bird's-eye view of the beautiful Catalonian landscape.

⑧ Boat Trips
Dofi Jet Boats: Blanes; 97 235 20 21; Boats every hour daily from Blanes and Lloret de Mar (twice daily from Calella); closed Oct–Mar; www. dofijetboats.com

Take a cruise from Calella and Blanes along the Costa Brava, stopping at the old town and medieval castle of Tossa de Mar.

⑨ Activities at the Canal Olímpic
Canal Olímpic: Av Canal Olímpic, Castelldefels; 93 636 28 96; www. canalolimpic.cat

Used for rowing competitions in the 1992 Olympics, the huge Canal Olímpic is now a leisure complex offering a host of activities.

⑩ Foraging for Mushrooms
Diputació de Barcelona: www.diba.cat

From late September to late October, Catalans flock to the hills in search of *bolets* – wild mushrooms. Some are poisonous, so amateurs should make sure they get a guide through the Diputació de Barcelona.

Places to Eat

PRICE CATEGORIES
For a three-course meal for one with half a bottle of wine (or equivalent meal), including taxes and extra charges.

€ under €35 ■ €€ €35–50 ■ €€€ over €50

1 Tragamar
Passatge Jimmy Rena s/n, Calella de Palafrugell ■ 97 261 43 36 ■ Closed Tue ■ €€
Book ahead for a table on the terrace or by one of the bay windows at this beachside restaurant, and enjoy stellar seafood dishes such as tuna carpaccio or lobster paella.

2 Les Cols
Mas les Cols, Ctra de la Canya s/n, Olot ■ 97 226 92 09 ■ Closed Sun D, Mon & Tue ■ www.lescols.com ■ €€€
Two-Michelin-starred Les Cols prepares contemporary Spanish cuisine with local seasonal produce in a stunning modern setting.

3 La Torre del Remei
Camí del Remei 3, Bolvir, Cerdanya ■ 97 214 01 82 ■ Closed Wed, Thu & Sun D, Mon & Tue ■ €€
A Modernista palace provides an elegant setting for wonderfully presented Catalan food.

4 Cal Ticus
C/Raval 19, Sant Sadurní d'Anoia ■ 93 818 41 60 ■ Closed Sun D, Mon–Thu ■ €
This modern restaurant serves traditional cuisine using seasonal products from nearby suppliers. A good selection of Penedès wines are on the list and for sale in their shop.

5 Fonda Europa
C/Anselm Clavé 1, Granollers ■ 93 870 03 12 ■ €€
Established in 1771, Fonda Europa was the first in a line of successful Catalan restaurants. Dishes include pig's trotters and a Catalan stockpot with meat and vegetables.

6 Lasal de Varador
Pg Marítim 1, Mataró ■ 93 114 05 80 ■ Closed Dec–Feb ■ €€
This beachfront restaurant serves tasty paellas, seafood and a range of other dishes, using organic and sustainably sourced ingredients.

7 Els Pescadors
Muelle Pesquero s/n, Arenys de Mar ■ 937 92 33 04 ■ Closed Sun D ■ €
Set inside the local *llotja* (wholesale fish market), this food spot serves fresh seafood. There are a few tables outside on the port overlooking the boats. Book ahead on the weekends.

8 Toc Al Mar
Pl d'Aiguablava, Begur ■ 972 11 32 32 ■ Closed Dec–Feb ■ www.tocalmar.cat
Located on a beach in Costa Brava, Toc Al Mar has tables on the sands. On offer is freshly grilled seafood, such as lobster, Palamós prawns, paella, black rice with squid ink and delicacies from the Mediterranean.

9 El Celler de Can Roca
C/Can Sunyer 48, Girona ■ 97 222 21 57 ■ Closed Sun, Mon, Tue L ■ www.cellercanroca.com ■ €€€
The Roca brothers' exciting Catalan cuisine is complemented by great wines. The restaurant has three Michelin stars and an 11-month waiting list. It is best to reserve ahead.

Prawn dish at El Celler

10 Cal Ton
C/Casal 8, Vilafranca del Penedès ■ 93 890 37 41 ■ Closed Mon, Tue D, Sun D, Easter, 3 weeks Aug ■ €€
Contemporary cuisine in the heart of Catalonia's biggest wine region. Order the *menu degustació*.

See map on pp124–5

Streetsmart

Looking down on the two entrance pavilions at Park Güell

Getting Around

Arriving by Air

Most flights arrive at **Barcelona El Prat Josep Tarradellas**, located 12 km (7.5 miles) southwest of the city centre. The airport has two terminals, linked by a shuttle bus. Local train services run every 30 minutes to the city centre, (about 25 mins), while metro Line 9 Sud links Zona Universitària station (Line 3) on the western side of the city (about 30 mins). There is also an express airport bus service, **Aerobús** (20–30 mins). Taxi ranks are located at both terminals (€30–40 into central Barcelona), as well as several car rental companies.

European budget airlines fly to Barcelona all year round. There are regular internal flights to local airports: Sabadell Airport, 20 km (12 miles) north of Barcelona, Lleida–Alguaire Airport, Reus Airport in Tarragona, Girona–Costa Brava Airport and Andorra–La Seu d'Urgell Airport.

Iberia offers a shuttle service between Madrid and Barcelona, with several flights a day, and also links to many other domestic destinations, as do **Vueling** and **Air Europa**. There are direct flights on national and low-cost airlines from the UK and most major European cities. Some low-cost and charter airlines also fly to Girona and Reus, both about 100 km (62 miles) away. There are direct flights from New York, Miami, Chicago, Washington DC and Atlanta, and flights from Australia and New Zealand via Dubai and other stopovers.

International Train Travel

Spain's rail services are operated by state-run **Renfe** (Red Nacional de Ferrocarriles Españoles). Buy your ticket on their website well ahead of travel, particularly for the peak summer season.

There are several routes to Spain from France. Trains from London, Brussels, Amsterdam, Geneva, Zürich and Milan reach Barcelona via Cerbère, on the French border with Catalonia. Direct, high-spreed luxury TALGO (Tren Articulado Ligero Goicoechea Oriol) trains, operated by Renfe, go to Barcelona from Paris, Milan, Geneva and Zürich. International trains arrive at Barcelona's Sants mainline station.

Sants offers a number of facilities, including lockers, ATMs and bureaux de change,

Domestic Train Travel

The fastest intercity services are the TALGO and AVE (operated by Renfe), which link Madrid with Barcelona in three hours. Private train operators Ouigo, Iryo and the Renfe subsidiary Avlo also run high-speed trains between Barcelona and Madrid. AVE routes link Barcelona with Seville and Málaga in five and a half hours. The *largo recorrido* (long-distance) trains are cheap but so slow that you usually need to travel overnight. *Regionales y cercanías* (regional and local services) are frequent and cheap. Overnight trains are offered by Estrella (a basic service) to Madrid, and by Trenhotel (more sophisticated) to A Coruña and Vigo, in Galicia.

Long-Distance Bus Travel

Often the cheapest way to reach and travel around Spain is by coach.

Spain has no national coach company; private regional companies operate routes around the country. The largest is **Alsa**, with routes and services covering most of Spain. Tickets and information are available at all main coach stations and on company websites.

Buses from towns and cities in Spain arrive at Estació del Nord and Sants. Several companies run day trips or longer tours around Catalonia. **Turisme de Catalunya** has details of trips.

Public Transport

Most towns and cities in Catalonia only offer a bus service, but the larger cities operate multiple public transport systems, including trams. Barcelona **Girona**, **Tarragona** and **Lleida** all have cheap and efficient bus services. Barcelona also has a well-run metro system. For up-todate information about public transport, as well as ticket advice, check out municipal websites.

TMB (Transports Metropolitans de Barcelona) runs the extensive public transport network in Barcelona and the suburbs. TMB has a useful interactive website, as well as an app. Both provide travel information, route finders, maps and schedules. Metro maps are also available at stations, while bus maps are available at the bigger tourist offices.

Tickets

A range of tickets and money-saving travel cards are available to tourists. Some cover train, bus and metro. Combined tickets allow you to hop from metro to FGC to bus lines without having to pay again. The *senzill* ticket, for a single journey, is €2.40 and can be used on metro, bus and FGC; the T-Casual is €11.35 and is the most useful for tourists, allowing ten trips on metro, bus and FGC (these can be combined with a time limit of an hour and a half); T-Dia and T-Mes are for unlimited daily and monthly travel respectively; the T-50/30 is for 50 journeys in 30 days on metro, bus and FGC.

For tourists, there are two-, three-, four- and five-day Hola Barcelona travel cards available (€16.40, €23.80, €31 and €38.20 if bought online through TMB) – these offer unlimited journeys on the metro, FGC and bus. Hola Barcelona cards also include the metro supplement for trips to and from the airport.

Metro

There are 12 underground metro lines in Barcelona, run by TMB. Lines are identified by number and colour. Platform signs distinguish between trains and their direction by displaying the last station on the line. In the street, look for a sign bearing a red "M" on a white diamond background. The metro is usually the quickest way to get around the city, especially as all multijourney tickets are valid for the metro and FGC lines (in Zone 1), as well as on the bus and local Renfe services. A Renfe or FGC sign at a metro station indicates that it has a Renfe or FGC connection. Metro trains run from 5am to midnight from Monday to Thursday, to midnight on Sunday and weekday public holidays, from 5am to 2am on Friday and the day before a public holiday, and all night on Saturdays.

The L9 metro line connects the city with the airport, and it stops at terminals 1 and 2, but is only really useful if you are headed to the north or west of the city. An airport supplement is charged on this route, and you will not be able to use the T-10 or other standard transport passes. However, the Hola Barcelona pass includes the airport supplement and is accepted on this route.

Trams

Barcelona has two comprehensive tram networks, Trambaix (T1, T2, T3) and Trambesòs (T4, T5, T6), which run between 4:55am and 12:30am daily (each line has slightly different hours). They are operated by **TRAM** (check website for routes and schedules). Trams are a cheap and efficient way to travel, and are often more accessible than other modes of public transport for those with limited mobility or travelling with pushchairs.

DIRECTORY

ARRIVING BY AIR

Aerobús
w aerobusbarcelona.es

Air Europa
w aireuropa.com

Barcelona El Prat Josep Tarradellas
w aena.es

Iberia
w iberia.com

Vueling
w vueling.com

INTERNATIONAL TRAIN TRAVEL

Renfe
w renfe.com

LONG-DISTANCE BUS TRAVEL

Alsa
w alsa.es

Turisme de Catalunya
w catalunyaturisme.cat

PUBLIC TRANSPORT

Girona
w girona.cat

Lleida
w atmlleida.cat

Tarragona
w emtanemambtu.cat

TMB
w tmb.cat

TRAMS

TRAM
w tram.cat

Bus

Buses are the most common mode of public transport in Catalonia, but timetables can be erratic. Many services do not run after 10pm, but there are some night buses in the cities.

In Barcelona the main city buses are white and red. Bus numbers beginning with H (for horizontal) run from one side of the city to another and those beginning with V (vertical) run top to bottom; D is diagonal. The Nitbus service runs nightly from around 10:30pm to 5am. Bus maps are available from the main tourist office in Plaça de Catalunya and on the TMB (Transports Metropolitans de Barcelona; see p135) website and app.

The privately owned **Aerobús** runs between Plaça de Catalunya and El Prat airport. Public transport passes are not valid on the Aerobús.

Local Trains

Renfe's network of local trains, *rodalies* in Catalan (*cercanías* in Spanish), is useful for longer distances within Barcelona, particularly between the main train stations: Sants and Estació de França. They are also useful for short hops to Sitges or the northern coastal towns. Maps are displayed at stations, or are available on the Renfe website (see p135) and app. Trains run 5:30am to 11:30pm daily, but hours vary from line to line. **Ferrocarrils de la Generalitat de Catalunya (FGC)** is a network of suburban trains run by the Catalan Government in and around Barcelona. They are useful for trips to Tibidabo, Pedralbes and the Collserola neighbourhoods.

Taxis

Barcelona's taxis are yellow and black, displaying a green light when free. All taxis are metered and show a minimum fee at the start of a journey. Generally speaking, the journey starts with a flat fee and then increases depending on the distance travelled. Rates increase between 8pm and 8am, and there is a €2.10 surcharge from midnight to 6am Friday to Sunday and on public holidays. Surcharges usually apply for going to and from the airport, the port and major train stations. You can flag taxis in the street, or call **Radio Taxis**, **Taxi Ecològic**, **Barna Taxi**, or **Taxi Class** to order one. **Taxi Amic** has cars adapted for people with a disability, though these need to be booked a day ahead.

Driving

If you drive to Spain in your own car, you must carry the vehicle's registration document, a valid insurance certificate, a passport or a national identity card and your driving licence at all times. You must also display a sticker on the back of the car showing its country of registration.

Spain has two types of motorway: *autopistas*, (toll roads) and *autovías* (toll-free). You can establish whether a motorway is toll-free by the letters that prefix the number of the road: A = free motorway, AP = toll motorway.

Carreteras nacionales, Spain's main roads, have black-and-white signs and are designated by the letter N (Nacional) plus a number. *Carreteras comarcales*, secondary roads, have a number preceded by the letter C.

Driving in Barcelona is not recommended. The narrow roads and one-way systems are tricky and parking can be difficult. The city has a pay-and-display system from 9am to 2pm and 4pm to 8pm Monday to Friday and all day Saturday. You can park in blue spaces for about €2–3 per hour. Tickets are valid for two hours but can be renewed. Green spaces are reserved for residents but can be used, if available, at a higher rate and are free at off-peak hours. At underground car parks, *lliure* means there is space, *complet* means full. Most are attended, but in automatic ones, you pay before returning to your car. Do not park where the pavement edge is yellow or where there is a private exit (*gual*). Blue and red signs saying "1–15" or "16–30" mean that you cannot park in the areas indicated on those dates of the month.

Driving to Barcelona

Many people drive to Catalonia via France. The most direct routes across the Pyrenees are the motorways through

Hendaye in the west and La Jonquera in the east. Port Bou is on a coastal route, while other routes snake over the top, entering Catalonia via the Val d'Aran, Andorra and Puigcerdà in the Cerdanya. From the UK, car ferries run from Plymouth to Santander and from Portsmouth to Santander and Bilbao.

Car Rental

The most popular car-rental companies are **Avis**, **Europcar** and **Hertz**. All have offices at airports, major train stations and in the larger cities.

Rules of the Road

Most traffic regulations and warnings to motorists are represented on signs by easily recognized symbols. To turn left at a busy junction or across oncoming traffic, you may have to turn right first and cross a main road, often by way of traffic lights, a bridge or underpass. If you are accidentally going in the wrong direction on a motorway or a main road with a solid white line, turn round at a sign for a *cambio de sentido*. At crossings, give way to the right unless a sign indicates otherwise.

Cycling

Barcelona has a growing network of cycle lanes that provide access to all the major sights of the city. There are a number of cycle-hire shops, including **Budget Bikes** and **Un Cotxe Menys**. Maps are available at these shops. Keep to cycle paths in the city centre, as cycling on roads can be unsafe.

Bicing, the municipal government-run free service, can be used with a Bicing card and supplies maps of the city's cycle lanes. Though this system is currently open to residents only, commercial operators offer rentals to visitors from around €10 for two hours to €60 for a week.

Many bike rental places also conduct cycling tours of the city. **Bike Tours Barcelona** has several themed tours, including a Modernista cycling tour and a beach tour, while **Steel Donkey** focuses on the quirky side of Barcelona. You can also explore the streets on a vintage-style Ural motor-cycle and sidecar with **Bright Side Tours**.

Walking

Most areas are best seen on foot, especially the old town and Gràcia, where a leisurely stroll is the only way to soak up the architectural and cultural riches. The seafront, from Port Vell to Port Olímpic, is also great for walking.

Try one of the excellent themed walking tours offered by the Barcelona Turisme office *(see p141)*. Their website offers an overview of the available tours, plus a discount if you buy them online.

Fans of Modernista architecture can book onto Barcelona Turisme's Modernista walking tour, which visits the main sites in the Eixample area, or pick up the free **Ruta del Modernisme** map at the tourist office.

(see p141)

DIRECTORY

BUS

Aerobús
w aerobusbarcelona.es

LOCAL TRAINS

Ferrocarrils de la Generalitat de Catalunya (FGC)
w fgc.cat

TAXIS

Barna Taxi
w barnataxi.com

Radio Taxis
w radiotaxi033.com

Taxi Amic
w taxi-amic.cat

Taxi Class
w taxiclassrent.com

Taxi Ecològic
w taxiecologic.com

CAR RENTAL

Avis
w avis.com

Europcar
w europcar.com

Hertz
w hertz.com

CYCLING

Bicing
w bicing.barcelona

Bike Tours Barcelona
w biketoursbarcelona.com

Bright Side Tours
w brightsidetours.com

Budget Bikes
w budgetbikes.eu

Steel Donkey
w steeldonkeybiketours.com

Un Cotxe Menys
w biketoursbarcelona.com

WALKING

Ruta del Modernisme
w rutadelmodernisme.com

Practical Information

Passports and Visas

For entry requirements, including visas, consult your nearest Spanish embassy or check the Spanish government's **Exteriores** and **Spain Travel Health** websites.

From late 2023, citizens of the UK, US, Canada, Australia and New Zealand do not need a visa for stays of up to three months, but must apply in advance for the European Travel Information and Authorization System **(ETIAS)**. EU nationals do not need a visa or an ETIAS. For those arriving from other countries, check with your local Spanish embassy or on the Spanish government's Exteriores website.

Government Advice

Now more than ever, it is important to consult both your and the Spanish government's advice before travelling. The **UK Foreign, Commonwealth & Development Office (FCDO)**, the **US Department of State**, the **Australian Department of Foreign Affairs and Trade** and the Spanish government's Exteriores website offer the latest information on security, health and local regulations.

Customs Information

You can find information on the laws relating to goods and currency taken in or out of Spain on the **Turespaña** (Spain's national tourist board) website.

For EU citizens there are no limits on most goods carried in or out of Spain, as long as they are only for personal use. Exceptions include weapons, some types of food and plants, and endangered species. Limits vary if travelling outside the EU, so always check restrictions before travelling. Non-EU residents can claim back VAT on EU purchases *(see p141)*.

Insurance

We recommend that you take out a comprehensive insurance policy covering theft, loss of belongings, medical care, cancellations and delays, and read the small print carefully.

EU citizens are eligible for free emergency medical care in Spain provided they have a valid European Health Insurance Card (EHIC) or UK Global Health Insurance Card **(GHIC)**.

Health

Spain has a world-class healthcare system. Emergency medical care in Spain is free for all EU and UK citizens. If you have an EHIC or GHIC, be sure to present this as soon as possible. You may have to pay after treatment and reclaim the money later.

For other visitors, payment of medical expenses is the patient's responsibility. It is therefore important to arrange comprehensive medical insurance before travelling.

No vaccinations are necessary for Spain.

Carry with you any prescriptions for medications that you take. Tap water is safe to drink unless stated otherwise.

For minor ailments, go to a *farmàcia* (pharmacy), identified by a red or green cross. When closed, they will post a sign giving the location of the nearest *farmàcia de guàrdia* that will be open. Pharmacies that are open 24 hours include the **Farmàcia Clapés** on La Rambla.

Smoking, Alcohol and Drugs

Smoking is banned in enclosed public spaces and is a fineable offence, although you can still smoke on the terraces of bars and restaurants.

Spain has a relaxed attitude towards alcohol consumption, but it is frowned upon to be openly drunk. In cities it is common to drink on the street outside the bar of purchase.

Most recreational drugs are illegal, and possession of even a very small quantity can lead to an extremely hefty fine. Amounts that suggest an intent to supply drugs to other people can lead to custodial sentences. Cannabis clubs can supply the drug to members, but it remains illegal to smoke it in public spaces.

ID

By law you must carry identification with you at all times in Spain. A photocopy of your passport should suffice. If stopped by the police, you may be asked to report to a police station with the original document.

Personal Security

Barcelona is a relatively safe city, although petty crimes such as pickpocketing and bag-snatching remain problematic. Usual safety precautions apply. Take particular care at markets, tourist sights and stations, and wear bags and cameras across your body, not on your shoulder. Be especially careful of pickpockets when get-ting on or off a crowded train or metro. Avoid walking alone in poorly lit areas.

To report a crime, go to the nearest *comissaria*. Although you may see police from other forces, contact is usually with the Mossos d'Esquadra, who wear navy blue uniforms.

Contact your embassy if you have your passport stolen, or in the event of a serious crime or accident.

The ambulance, police and fire brigade can be reached on the Europe-wide **emergency** number 112. There are also dedicated lines for the **Policía Nacional** (the national police force), the **Guàrdia Urbana** (the municipal police force), the **Mossos d'Esquadra** (the Catalonian police force) as well as for calling an **ambulance**.

As a rule, Catalans are very accepting of all people, regardless of their race, gender or sexuality. Homosexuality was legalized in 1979 and in 2007, Spain recognized the right to legally change your gender. If you do feel unsafe, the **Safe Space Alliance** pinpoints your nearest place of refuge.

Travellers with Specific Requirements

Spain's **COCEMFE** (Confederación Española de Personas con Discapacidad Física y Orgánica) provides useful information, while companies, such as **Tourism For All** and **Accessible Spain**, offer specialist tours for those with reduced mobility, sight and hearing.

Spain's public transport system generally caters for all passengers, with wheelchairs, adapted toilets, and reserved car parking available at airports and stations. Trains and some buses accommodate wheelchair-bound passengers. Metro maps in Braille are available from **ONCE** (Organización Nacional de Ciegos).

DIRECTORY

PASSPORTS AND VISAS

ETIAS
w etiasvisa.com

Exteriores
w exteriores.gob.es

Spain Travel Health
w spth.gob.es

GOVERNMENT ADVICE

Australian Department of Foreign Affairs and Trade
w smartraveller.gov.au

UK Foreign, Commonwealth & Development Office (FCDO)
w gov.uk/foreign-travel-advice

US Department of State
w travel.state.gov

CUSTOMS INFORMATION

Turespaña
w spain.info

INSURANCE

GHIC
w ghic.org.uk

HEALTH

Farmàcia Clapés
MAP L3 ■ La Rambla 98
w farmaciaclapes.com

PERSONAL SECURITY

Ambulance
c 061

Emergency
c 112

Guàrdia Urbana
c 092

Mossos d'Esquadra
c 112

Policía Nacional
c 091

Safe Space Alliance
w safespacealliance.com

TRAVELLERS WITH SPECIFIC REQUIREMENTS

Accessible Spain
w accessiblespaintravel.com

COCEMFE
w cocemfe.es

ONCE
w once.es

Tourism For All
w tourismforall.org.uk

Time Zone

Spain operates on Central European Time (CET), which is one hour ahead of Greenwich Mean Time (GMT) and six hours ahead of US Eastern Standard Time (EST). The clock moves forward one hour during daylight savings time, from the last Sunday in March until the last Sunday in November.

Money

Spain uses the euro (€). Most urban establishments accept major credit, debit and prepaid currency cards. Contactless payments are common in Barcelona, but it's a good idea to carry cash for smaller items. ATMs are widely available, although many charge for cash withdrawals. Tipping is not expected for hotel housekeeping, but porters will expect €1–2 per bag. Rounding up the fare to the nearest euro is expected by taxi drivers and it is usual to tip waiters 5–10 per cent.

Electrical Appliances

Spain uses plugs with two round pins and an electrical voltage and frequency of 230V/50Hz. North American devices will need adaptors and voltage converters.

Mobile Phones and Wi-Fi

Free Wi-Fi is reasonably common, particularly in libraries, large public spaces, restaurants and bars. Some places, such as airports and hotels, may charge for using their Wi-Fi. The city council provides free Wi-Fi around Barcelona. Use the **WiFi Map** website and app to find free Wi-Fi hotspots near you.

Visitors travelling to Spain with EU tariffs can use their devices abroad without being affected by roaming charges. Users will be charged the same rates for data, calls and texts as at home.

Postal Services

Main branches of Spain's **Correos** post offices are usually open 8:30am–8:30pm Monday to Friday and 9:30am–1pm on Saturdays. Suburban and village branches open 9am–2pm during the week and 9:30am–1pm Saturday. Mailboxes are painted bright yellow.

Weather

The climate is typically Mediterranean, with cool winters and warm summers. July can be hot and humid, with temperatures reaching 35° C (95° F). January and February are the two coldest months, although temperatures rarely drop below 10° C (50° F).

Opening Hours

Many shops and some museums and public buildings may close for the siesta, roughly between 1pm and 5pm. Larger shops and department stores don't close at lunchtime and are usually open until 9 or 10pm.

Many museums, public buildings and monuments are closed on Monday.

Opening hours for museums and galleries vary and may change with the season. It is best to check their websites before you visit.

On Sundays, churches and cathedrals will generally not permit visitors during Mass.

Most museums, public buildings and many shops close early or for the day on public holidays: New Year's Day, Epiphany (6 Jan), Good Friday, Easter Sunday, Feast of Sant Jordi (23 Apr), Labour Day (1 May), Feast of Sant Joan (24 Jun), Ascension Day (15 Aug), Catalan Day (11 Sep), Hispanic Day (12 Oct), All Saints' Day (1 Nov), Constitution Day (6 Dec), Immaculate Conception (8 Dec), Christmas Day (25 Dec), and the Feast of St Stephen (26 Dec).

The COVID-19 pandemic proved that situations can change suddenly. Always check before visiting attractions and hospitality venues for up-to-date hours and booking requirements.

Visitor Information

Multilingual staff give out free maps and information at the **Barcelona Turisme** main tourist information office at Plaça de Catalunya. They also have a useful accommodation booking service and bureau de change. There are additional Barcelona Turisme offices at the airport, La Rambla, Estació de Sants and Plaça de Sant Jaume, and booths at Estació del Nord, Plaça Espanya and other key tourist spots.

In summer, red-jacketed tourist information officers roam the busiest areas giving out maps and advice. Barcelona Turisme's excellent website provides information, sells tickets and lets you book accommodation. It also has useful apps, including a general guide to the city, as well as specific guides to Medieval Barcelona, Roman Barcelona and Gaudí's Barcelona.

Barcelona offers the **Barcelona Card**, a visitor's pass or discount card for exhibitions, events and museum entry, plus participating restaurants. This is not free, so consider carefully how many of the offers you are likely to take advantage of before purchasing a card.

The **Culture Institute** in the Palau de la Virreina offers information on cultural and arts events and a ticket-purchase service. The **Barcelona City Council's** website and the **Turisme de Catalunya** office as well as website are also good sources of information.

Useful apps include Moovit and Citymapper for route planning and transport information.

Local Customs

Regional pride is strong throughout Spain. Be wary of referring to Catalans as "Spanish", as this can sometimes cause offence.

A famous Spanish tradition is the siesta which sees many shops closing between 1pm and 5pm. This is not always observed by large stores or in very touristy areas.

It is wise to ensure that you are dressed modestly when visiting religious buildings, with knees and shoulders covered.

Language

The two official languages of Catalonia are *castellano* (Castilian Spanish) and Catalan. Almost every Catalan can speak Castilian Spanish, but most consider Catalan their first language. As a visitor, it is perfectly acceptable to speak Castilian wherever you are. English is widely spoken in the cities and other tourist spots, but not always in rural areas.

Taxes and Refunds

IVA (VAT) is normally 21 per cent, but with lower rates for certain goods and services, such as hotels and restaurants. Under certain conditions, non-EU citizens can claim a rebate of these taxes. Retailers can give you a form to fill out, which you can then present to a customs officer with your receipts as you leave. If the shop offers DIVA, you can fill that form out instead and validate it automatically at selfservice machines found in the airport.

Accommodation

Catalonia offers a range of accommodation, including government-run hotels called

paradors. A useful list of accommodation can be found on the **Turespaña** website. Try to book your accommodation well in advance if you plan to visit in the peak season (July and August). Rates are also higher during major fiestas. Most hotels quote prices without including tax (IVA), which is 10 per cent. In Barcelona, visitors must pay a nightly tax that varies from €2.75 to €5.25 depending on the number of stars of the hotel. There is a seven-day maximum.

DIRECTORY

MOBILE PHONES AND WI-FI

WiFi Map
Ⓦ wifimap.io

POSTAL SERVICES

Correos
Ⓦ correos.es

VISITOR INFORMATION

Barcelona Card
Ⓦ bcnshop.barcelona turisme.com/shopv3/en/product/1/barcelona-card.html

Barcelona City Council
Ⓦ barcelona.cat

Barcelona Turisme
MAP M1 ■ Pl de Catalunya 17
Ⓦ barcelonaturisme.com

Catalunya Turisme
Ⓦ catalunyaturisme.cat

Culture Institute
MAP L3 ■ La Rambla 99
Ⓒ 93 316 10 00

Turisme de Catalunya
MAP E2 ■ Palau Robert, Pg de Gràcia 107
Ⓦ catalunya.com

ACCOMMODATION

Turespaña
Ⓦ spain.info

Places to Stay

PRICE CATEGORIES

For a standard double room per night (with breakfast if included), including taxes and extra charges.

€ under €120   €€ €120–240   €€€ over €240

Luxury Hotels

Granados 83

MAP E2 ■ C/Enric Granados 83 ■ 93 492 96 70 ■ www.hotel granados83.com ■ €€
Rooms at this designer hotel are decorated with African zebrawood, chocolate brown leather and original pieces of Hindu and Buddhist art. Suites have private terraces that overlook a plunge pool. There is a restaurant, and a pretty rooftop pool with a fashionable bar.

ABaC Restaurant and Hotel

MAP B1 ■ Av Tibidabo 1 ■ 93 319 66 00 ■ www. abacbarcelona.com ■ €€€
This boutique hotel, set in a listed building, has luxury amenities perfectly suited for the smaller number of guests. The 17 gorgeous rooms are stylishly decorated in a contemporary, minimal style. There is a wellness spa with a hammam and Jacuzzi, plus a small garden. It also has one of the city's finest restaurants, ABaC, which earned its chef Jordi Cruz three Michelin stars.

Alma Barcelona

MAP E2 ■ C/Mallorca 271 ■ 93 216 44 90 ■ www.almahotels. com/barcelona ■ €€€
This hotel exudes elegance and is renowned for its excellent service. Several original 19th-century details have been preserved, but the rooms are chic and minimalist. The glorious garden (see p61) and the roof terrace are ideal for relaxing after a day's sightseeing.

Almanac Hotel

MAP E3 ■ Gran Via de les Corts Catalanes 619 ■ 93 216 44 90 ■ www. almanachotels.com ■ €€€
A plush luxury hotel kitted out by top local designer Jaime Beriestain, who took an Art Deco ethos to fashionable heights with velvety textiles, fine noble wood and brass fittings. Here, smooth elegance is complemented by premium service. The rooftop sundeck and pool are as spectacular as one would expect for the price, the silver service breakfast is unmatched, and each room has an enclosed balcony where guests can snuggle up on a day bed.

Casa Camper

MAP L2 ■ C/Elisabets 11 ■ 93 342 62 80 ■ www. casacamper.com ■ €€€
A converted 19th-century mansion, this hotel is filled with innovative yet comfortable design touches. It has stylish rooms, a roof terrace, an extraordinary vertical garden and a free 24-hour bar. The Dos Palillos restaurant is run by Albert Raurich, former chef at El Bulli. Well-deserving of its Michelin star, it specializes in creative, tapas-style Asian dishes.

El Palace Barcelona Hotel

MAP F3 ■ Gran Via de les Corts Catalanes 668 ■ 93 510 11 30 ■ www. hotelpalacebarcelona. com ■ €€€
With its 1919 Neo-Classical façade, grand public areas and excellent service, this hotel is synonymous with tradition and style. Its restaurant is a temple to the freshest seafood, with award-winning chef Rafa Zafra at the helm. The rooftop bistro pairs casually creative plates with unforgettable views.

Grand Hotel Central

MAP E4 ■ Via Laietana 30 ■ 93 295 79 00 ■ www. grandhotelcentral.com ■ €€€
Large, elegant hotel located close to the Barri Gòtic and El Born. It has accommodating staff, a fitness centre and an elegant restaurant serving excellent Mediterranean cuisine. But the highlight is the hotel's stunning rooftop infinity pool, which provides spectacular views of the city.

Hotel Arts Barcelona

MAP G5 ■ C/Marina 19–21 ■ 93 221 10 00 ■ www.hotelarts barcelona.com ■ €€€
The ne plus ultra of the city's five-star hotels, this hotel is located a few steps

rom the sea, with large ooms and top-notch laces to dine. Enoteca, un by Catalan chef Paco Pérez (of the Costa Brava's Miramar restaurant), offers imaginative Mediterranean cuisine nd has been awarded wo Michelin stars. The utoor pool on the first loor has fantastic views.

Majestic Hotel nd Spa

MAP E2 ■ Pg de Gràcia 68 ■ 93 488 17 17 ■ https:// majestichotelgroup.com ■ €€€

aultless service and tately decor are the allmarks of this aptly amed hotel. Exit through he reassuringly heavy rass-and-glass doors nd you'll find yourself ust a few steps from he Modernista gems f Eixample. The rooftop lunge pool has great iews of the Barcelona ityscape and Gaudí's ncredible masterpiece, he Sagrada Família.

W Barcelona

MAP E5 ■ Pl de la Rosa els Vents 1 ■ 93 295 8 00 ■ www.w-arcelona.cat ■ €€€ opularly known as he Hotel Vela ("Sail lotel"), thanks to its autically billowing form nd location right next to he water, this lavishly ppointed five-star option njoys unparalleled sea iews. With its massive oor-to-ceiling windows : is not hard to imagine ou are at sea. The hotel as all the usual luxury xtras, from a stunning utdoor pool and 7,500-q-ft (700-sq-m) spa o four designer bars nd restaurants.

Historic Hotels

Hotel Duquesa de Cardona

MAP M6 ■ Pg Colón 12 ■ 93 268 90 90 ■ www. hduquesadecardona.com ■ €€

The 16th-century home of the noble Cardona family used to host the royal court on its visits to the city. Now a stylish hotel, it combines the original structure with avant-garde decor and modern facilities. The rooftop terrace has a plunge pool and great views over the Port Vell area.

Hotel España

MAP L4 ■ C/Sant Pau 9 ■ 93 550 00 00 ■ www. hotelespanya.com ■ €€ This little gem of Catalan *Modernisme* is set in an 1850 building renovated in 1903 by Modernista architect Lluís Domènech i Montaner, artist Ramón Casas and sculptor Eusebi Arnau, who carved the splendid alabaster fireplace. There is a roof-top pool and solarium, and the Fonda España restaurant is run by Michelin-starred chef Martín Berasategui.

Praktik Rambla

MAP E3 ■ Rambla de Catalunya 27 ■ 93 343 66 90 ■ www.hotelpraktik rambla.com ■ €€ The centrally located budget hotel is set in a Modernista mansion. It combines traditional and avant-garde decor. The original tiling and carved woodwork from the 20th century make a striking contrast with the contemporary furnishings. The hotel has an outdoor terrace and also provides

free Wi-Fi. Book in advance as there are only a few rooms.

Casa Fuster

MAP E1 ■ Pg de Gràcia 132 ■ 93 255 30 00 ■ www.hotelcasafuster. com ■ €€€ Originally designed by Domènech i Montaner, whose works have been declared World Heritage Sites by the UNESCO. This hotel is one of the city's most prestigious and luxurious. The Modernista details have been retained, but elegantly fused with 21st-century amenities.

Gran Hotel La Florida

MAP B1 ■ Ctra Vallvidrera al Tibidabo 83–93 ■ 93 259 30 00 ■ www.hotel floridabarcelona.com ■ €€€ Set in a Modernista villa high up in the hills in Tibidabo, this luxurious hotel has maintained its legen-dary views over the city since 1924, when it was built for Dr. Andreu, pharmaceutical entre-preneur and philanthropist. Converted into a hotel in 1950, its guests have included Ernest Hemingway, Princess Fabiola and the prince of Belgium.

Hotel 1898

MAP L2 ■ La Rambla 109 ■ 93 552 95 52 ■ www. hotel1898.com ■ €€€ This chic hotel has retained some of the building's original fittings, such as the 20th-century revolving door, and added modern amenities, such as a swimming pool, a fitness centre and spa, and a good restaurant.

Hotel Claris

MAP E2 ▪ C/Pau Claris 150 ▪ 93 487 62 62 ▪ www.hotelclaris.com ▪ €€€

This 19th-century palace was once home to the Counts of Vedruna. It has a small collection of Pre-Columbian art, some objects from which also decorate the suites. Guests can relax at the Mayan spa and cool off in the rooftop plunge pool.

Hotel Neri

MAP M3 ▪ C/Sant Sever 5 ▪ 93 310 96 55 ▪ www.hotelneri.com ▪ €€€

This 17th-century former palace at the heart of the Barri Gòtic offers an exclusive combination of history, the avant-garde and glamour. There is a library, a solarium and a roof terrace with views to the cathedral.

Mercer Hotel

MAP N4 ▪ C/Lledó 7 ▪ 93 310 74 80 ▪ www.mercerbarcelona.com ▪ €€€

This boutique hotel in the old part of town has 28 large, comfortable rooms and the decor has a cutting-edge, designer feel to it. You can take in the amazing views of the city from the swimming pool on the roof terrace. There is also a cocktail bar and restaurant.

Monument

MAP E2 ▪ Pg de Gràcia 75 ▪ 93 548 20 00 ▪ www.monumenthotel.com ▪ €€€

An old neo-Gothic palace right on the posh Passeig de Gràcia has been converted to a luxury hotel with an arty feel, including some bold contemporary design pieces. Guests can choose the street-facing rooms or the rear ones, which look out onto a typical Eixample courtyard.

Central Stays

chic&basic Born

MAP P4 ▪ C/Princesa 50 ▪ 93 295 46 52 ▪ www.chicandbasic.com ▪ €€

This 19th-century town house is a big hit with fashionistas. Rooms are minimalist with contemporary glass and steel bathrooms and colourful LED lights. Bike hire and activities such as stand-up paddle board are on offer, and there's a common area where you can mingle with other guests.

Casa Bonay

MAP F3 ▪ Gran Via de les Corts Catalanes 700 ▪ 93 545 80 70 ▪ https://casabonay.com ▪ €€

Effortlessly stylish and hip urban hangout Casa Bonay is exquisitely decorated. Rooms come in a range of sizes, while amenities include a roof terrace and a huge café-and-bar (on the ground floor). The hotel promises a relaxed vibe.

Hotel Colón

MAP N3 ▪ Av de la Catedral 7 ▪ 93 301 14 04 ▪ https://hotelcolonbarcelona.es ▪ €€

A family-owned Barri Gòtic hotel, the Colón has traditional decor with mirrors and oil paintings throughout. The magnificent views of the cathedral and Plaça de la Seu are stunning. Hotel guests have included Sartre, Arata Isozaki and Joan Miró, who made this place his home in the 1960 and 70s.

Hotel Constanza

MAP F3 ▪ C/Bruc 33 ▪ 93 270 19 10 ▪ www.hotelconstanza.com ▪ €€

This elegant mid-sized hotel is near Eixample's main sights. Some of the stylish rooms come with terraces. The adjoining Bruc 33 restaurant serves homemade tapas and Mediterranean specialities.

Hotel Jazz

MAP L1 ▪ C/Pelai 3 ▪ 93 552 96 96 ▪ www.hoteljazz.com ▪ €€

The modern Hotel Jazz may not be the most characterful option, but it is centrally located and has several amenities, including a small rooftop pool. It is great value for money, and the friendly staff are always on hand to offer help and advice.

Hotel Soho Barcelona

MAP D3 ▪ Gran Vía Corts Catalanes 543 ▪ 93 552 96 10 ▪ www.hotelsohobarcelona.com ▪ €€

Top Spanish architect Alfredo Arribas designed this stylish, contemporary hotel. Located in the heart of Eixample, it's perfect for shopping, sightseeing and enjoying the nightlife. The rooftop pool has magnificent views.

Park Hotel

MAP F5 ▪ Av Marquès de l'Argentera 11 ▪ 93 319 60 00 ▪ www.parkhotelbarcelona.com ▪ €€

A 1950s design classic with a gorgeous wrap-around staircase, the Park Hotel was redone by the original architect's son. Rooms are small but comfortably furnished, and some have balconies. It is located near the fashionable Born clubs and boutiques.

Room Mate Emma

MAP E2 ■ C/Rosselló 205 ■ 93 238 56 06 ■ https://room-matehotels.com/en/emma ■ €€

A great option if you're looking for style on a budget, the Room Mate Emma offers compact but gorgeously designed bedrooms in the very centre of the city. There's no restaurant, but there is a buffet breakfast on offer.

Mandarin Oriental Barcelona

MAP E3 ■ Pg de Gràcia 38–40 ■ 93 151 88 88 ■ www.mandarinorien al.es/barcelona/passeig-de-gracia/luxury-hotel ■ €€€

This ultra-luxurious hotel has rooms overlooking either the iconic Passeig de Gràcia or the gorgeous interior gardens. It has a spa and a roof terrace with a splash pool. With two Michelin stars, the gourmet restaurant, Moments, serves exquisite Catalan dishes made by renowned chef Carme Ruscalleda – of Sant Pau fame *(see p131)* – and her son Raül Balam.

Sofitel Barcelona Skipper

MAP G6 ■ Av Litoral 10 ■ 93 221 65 65 ■ www.sullman-barcelona-skipper.com ■ €€€

Overlooking the sea close to the beach, the Skipper is the perfect spot for a summer city break. Ideal for business travellers, it has all the facilities guests would expect of a five-star hotel. Weekend bargains are often available.

Mid-Range Hotels

Circa 1905

MAP E2 ■ C/Provença 286 ■ 93 505 69 60 ■ www.circa1905.com ■ €€

This is one of a new breed of boutique B&Bs, and has just nine rooms (one with a private terrace) in a charming Modernista mansion. Furnished with a tasteful mix of antique and contemporary pieces, it has an elegant lounge where you can leaf through the books and enjoy a drink. Long-term rates available.

H10 Art Gallery

MAP E2 ■ C/Enric Granados 62 ■ 932 14 20 30 ■ www.h10hotels. com ■ €€

Colourful, contemporary and very chic, H10 Art Gallery has a beautiful interior patio and a rooftop terrace with a plunge pool. Rooms are bright and minimalist, and each floor draws inspiration from a different artist, from Miró to Lichtenstein. It's on one of Barcelona's prettiest streets, and has its own restaurant and café-bar.

Hotel Barcelona Catedral

MAP M3 ■ C/Capellans 4 ■ 93 304 22 55 ■ www. barcelonacatedral.com ■ €€

Enjoy phenomenal views over the Barri Gòtic from the roof terrace at this modern hotel, which also has a rooftop plunge pool and a small fitness room. The guest rooms are spacious and bright, the service excellent, and the off-season prices a bargain. The hotel offers free bike hire, and conducts complimentary walking tours through the quarter on Wednesdays and Sundays.

Sonder Casa Luz

MAP E3 ■ Ronda de Universitat 1 ■ 93 002 25 05 ■ https://hotel casaluz.com ■ €€

Set in an elegant 19th-century building, this boutique hotel offers chic rooms, some with a private terrace. There is also a beautiful rooftop bar with scenic views over the skyline.

Hotel Ciutat Vella

MAP L1 ■ C/Tallers 66 ■ 934 81 37 99 ■ www. hotelciutatvella.com ■ €€

Offering modern rooms decorated in warm colours, this great value option is located just a 5-minute walk from La Rambla. Some rooms have small terraces, and there is a plunge pool and sun deck on the roof.

Hotel Granvía

MAP F3 ■ Gran Vía de les Corts Catalanes 642 ■ 93 318 19 00 ■ www. hotelgranvia.com ■ €€

This opulent late 19th-century mansion, built for a Barcelona philanthropist, has a domed stained-glass entrance, a fairy-tale staircase and lavish stucco ceilings. The rooms have understated modern decor, and there is a charming hidden patio garden at the back.

For a key to hotel price categories see p142

Musik Boutique Hotel
MAP P3 ▪ C/Sant Pere Més Baix 62 ▪ 93 222 55 44 ▪ www.musikboutique hotel.com ▪ €€
Close to the magnificent Palau de la Música, this small and welcoming hotel has a contemporary, interior behind an 18th-century façade. The largest of the rooms have private terraces.

Primero Primera
MAP B1 ▪ C/Doctor Carulla 25–29 ▪ 93 417 56 00 ▪ www.primero primera.com ▪ €€
This plush hotel in the upmarket Sant Gervasi area combines vintage chic with contemporary sophistication. There's a cosy lounge with an open fire and leather armchairs and a romantic little garden with a small pool and sun loungers.

Villa Emilia
MAP C3 ▪ C/Calàbria 115 ▪ 93 252 52 85 ▪ www. hotelvillaemilia.com ▪ €€
Slightly off the beaten track, but close to the hip Sant Antoni neighbourhood, which is packed with bars and boutiques, this friendly hotel offers stylish rooms and a roof terrace for barbecues in summer and cocktails under heaters in winter. The lobby bar has regular jazz concerts.

Violeta Boutique
MAP F3 & N1 ▪ C/Caspe 38 ▪ 93 302 81 58 ▪ https:// violetaboutique.com ▪ €€
Each of the spacious rooms at this lovely guesthouse has been individually decorated, and guests can sit out on a pretty balcony with a drink or the newspaper.

They also offer a smart penthouse apartment which has its own kitchen and terrace.

Budget Hotels

chic&basic Zoo
MAP Q4 ▪ Pg Picasso 22 ▪ 93 295 46 52 ▪ www. chicandbasic.com ▪ €
Part of the chic&basic chain, this small hotel is located in a historic building in the heart of the Born district, opposite Parc de la Ciutadella. The largest rooms have balconies facing the park.

El Jardí
MAP M3 ▪ Pl Sant Josep Oriol 1 ▪ 93 301 59 00 ▪ www.eljardi.com ▪ €
In the snug heart of the Barri Gòtic, this hostel has simple, spotless en suite rooms done up in light wood and cool colours. The bright breakfast room has balconies overlooking the square.

Hostal Goya
MAP N1 ▪ C/Pau Claris 74 ▪ 93 302 25 65 ▪ www.hostalgoya. com ▪ €
This well-run hostel was established in 1952. The rooms are bright and modern, with some designer touches. Most have en suite bathrooms, but only some have air conditioning.

Hostal Oliva
MAP E3 ▪ Pg de Gràcia 32 ▪ 93 488 01 62 ▪ www. hostaloliva.com ▪ €
From the the individually wrapped soaps to the lovely vintage elevator, this cheerful, family-run hostel is one of the city's best. The beautiful Modernista building has

airy rooms, some with en suite bathrooms.

Market
MAP D3 ▪ Comte Borrell 68 ▪ 93 325 12 05 ▪ www. hotelmarketbarcelona. com ▪ €
Close to the Modernista Sant Antoni market, the rooms in this stylish hotel have an airy feel, with glossy lacquered wood and a red, white and black colour scheme. Book well in advance.

Motel One Barcelona-Ciutadella
MAP Q3 ▪ Passeig de Pujades 11–13 ▪ 93 626 19 00 ▪ €
Offering glorious views of the Ciutadella Park, this hotel is perfect for those travelling on a budget. The rooms, some with balconies, are decorated in cheery teal and aqua tones, and the leafy terrace is a dreamy spot in which to relax.

Praktik Vinoteca
MAP E3 ▪ C/Balmes 51 ▪ 93 454 50 28 ▪ www. hotelpraktikvinoteca.com ▪ €
Ideal if you're looking for style on a budget, this wine-themed boutique hotel in Eixample has small but well-designed rooms. You can enjoy a wide range of local wines – over 900 or so on display – in the elegant and inviting lobby bar, and there's also a miniature terrace backed by plants.

Sol y k
MAP M5 ▪ C/Cervantes 2 ▪ 655 566 506 ▪ https:// www.solyk.net ▪ €
A budget option in the heart of the Barri Gòtic. A handful of individually

decorated rooms with mosaic headboards and original art set the Sol y k apart from other guest-houses. Some rooms have en suites.

Hostal La Palmera

MAP E4 ■ C/Jerusalem 31 ■ 93 667 02 48 ■ €
Conveniently located directly behind the Boqueria market, this friendly, family-run hostel offers a range of bright and simply decorated rooms, all with air conditioning. There is also a choice of private or shared bathrooms, a 24/7 reception and reliable Wi-Fi throughout.

Hotel Brummell

MAP 5C ■ C/Nou de la Rambla 174 ■ 93 125 86 22 ■ www.hotel brummell.com ■ €€
A stylish little charmer in lively Poble Sec, this hotel has a rooftop sun deck and plunge pool to go with the contemporarily styled rooms. Complimentary yoga classes, a sauna and a courtyard filled with plants make it the perfect city oasis.

Campsites and Aparthotels

Aparthotel Atenea

C/Joan Güell 207–211 ■ 93 490 66 40 ■ www. aparthotelatenea. com ■ €
Designed with business travellers in mind, this top-notch aparthotel is sited near the business and financial district around upper Diagonal. Rooms are spacious and well equipped, and there are several conference rooms and a 24-hour laundry service.

Aparthotel Bertran

C/de Bertran 150 ■ 93 212 75 50 ■ www. bertran-hotel.com ■ €
This accommodation has generous studios and apartments (many with balconies), a rooftop swimming pool, a small gym and 24-hour laundry service. Breakfast is served in your apartment.

Cala Llevadó

Ctra GI-682 km 18.9, Tossa de Mar ■ 97 234 03 14 ■ Closed Oct–Easter ■ https://cala llevado.com ■ €
A well-kept, eco-friendly campsite on the Costa Brava near the beautiful beach of Tamariu. It is just 200 m (656 ft) from the beach and within walking distance of the town for bars, restaurants and grocery shops. The campsite has a picturesque location by the sea, with palm-shaded pitches for tents. Great for families.

Camping Barcelona

Ctra N-II, km 650, 8 km (5 miles) E of Mataró ■ 93 790 47 20 ■ Closed Nov–Mar ■ www.camping barcelona.com ■ €
Located 28 km (17 miles) north of Barcelona, this is set next to a small beach. Bungalows are available to rent as are pitches.

Camping Globo Rojo

Ctra N-II km 660, 9, Canet de Mar ■ 93 794 11 43 ■ Closed Oct–Mar ■ www.globo-rojo.com ■ €
Close to the beaches of Canet de Mar, Globo Rojo offers pitches, mobile homes, bungalows and other accommodation units. There is a pool, tennis court and

football pitch. Great for kids. Direct bus and train to Barcelona.

Camping Masnou Barcelona

C/Camil Fabra 33 (N-II, km 663), El Masnou ■ 93 555 15 03 ■ www. campingmasnou barcelona.com ■ €
Family-owned campsite located 11 km (7 miles) north of Barcelona and close to the El Masnou train station, which is a 20-minute journey from the city. The site faces the sea and has a small beach close by. They offer shaded pitches as well as rooms. Facilities include a pool, a supermarket and a terrace bar with Wi-Fi.

Camping Roca Grossa

Ctra N-II km 665, Calella ■ 93 769 12 97 ■ Closed Oct–Mar ■ www.roca grossa.com ■ €
Positioned between the mountains and the sea, this modern, family-oriented campsite has good installations and access to the nearby beach. It has a large swimming pool, a restaurant and bar and is only 1 km (0.6 mile) from the lively resort of Calella. Both pitches and bungalows are available.

Camping Sitges

Ctra Comarcal C-246a, km 38, Sitges ■ 93 894 10 80 ■ Closed mid-Oct–mid-March ■ www.camping sitges.com ■ €
This is a small, well-kept campsite with a swimming pool, playground and a supermarket. It is located 2 km (1 mile) south of Sitges, and close to its renowned beaches.

For a key to hotel price categories see p142

Sant Jordi Sagrada Família

MAP E2 ▪ C/Freser 5
▪ 93 446 05 17 ▪ www.
santjordihostels.com ▪ €
The Sant Jordi group's
most comfortable accom-
modation in Barcelona,
this features a skate-
board theme, complete
with a mini-ramp. Guests
can choose from rooms,
dorms as well as private
apartments for their stay.

Citadines

MAP L2 ▪ La Rambla 122
▪ 93 270 11 11 ▪ www.
citadines.com ▪ €€
If you're smitten with the
city, try an aparthotel for
a longer stay. This one
on La Rambla has well-
appointed studios and
small apartments with
a kitchenette, iron and
CD stereo. The rooftop
terrace has beach chairs
and showers and is just
the spot to unwind.

Suites Avenue

MAP E2 ▪ Pg de Gràcia 83
▪ 93 272 37 16 ▪ www.
suitesavenue.com ▪ €€€
These apartments set
on Barcelona's grandest
avenue, are housed in
a striking building with
a rippling façade. The
chic, minimalist design
is complemented by
artworks and numerous
antiquities. The amenities
include a spa area and
a stunning terrace with a
plunge pool.

Hostels

Be Dream Hostel Barcelona

Av Alfonso XIII 28b,
Badalona ▪ 93 399 14 20
▪ www.behostels.com/
dream ▪ €
A 20-minute metro ride
from the city centre, but
close to the beaches,
this hostel is well priced,
with rooms and dorms
sleeping between 2 and
12 guests. Kitchen as
well as laundry facilities
are included.

Fabrizzio's Petit

MAP F3 ▪ C/Bruc 65, 2–2
▪ 93 215 40 59 ▪ www.
fabrizzios.com ▪ €
Choose from either
simple rooms or dorms
at this friendly hostel,
which also has a terrace,
a kitchen and a lounge.
The staff arrange all sorts
of activities, including
communal dinners,
walking tours and
other events.

Feetup Garden House Hostel

C/ d'Hedilla 58 ▪ 93 427
24 79 ▪ https://feetup
hostels.com ▪ €
This friendly hostel is
located on the outskirts
of the city, near Gaudí's
beautiful Park Güell. It's
only a 15-minute metro
ride into the centre of
town. There is a lovely
garden and roof terrace,
and a relaxed vibe.

INOUT Hostel

C/Major del Rectoret 2,
Vallvidrera ▪ 93 280 09 85
▪ www.inouthostel.com
▪ €
Located at a 12-minute
train ride from the city
centre in the forest-filled
enclave Vallvidrera, INOUT
Hostel is an admirable
enterprise that provides
employment to people
who are differently-abled.
Nearly 90 per cent of their
work force consists of
people with specific needs.
Rooms accommodate four
to ten people. There are
sports facilities as well
as a pool here.

Itaca Hostel

MAP N3 ▪ C/Ripoll 21
▪ 93 301 97 51 ▪ www.
itacahostel.com ▪ €
Located in the heart of
the Barri Gòtic Quarter,
this hostel has space for
30 guests in double rooms,
dorms (for up to 6 people)
and apartments. Bedding
and lockers are included
in the price and there is
Wi-Fi available in the
main building.

Kabul Party Hostel

MAP L4 ▪ Pl Reial 17
▪ 93 318 51 90 ▪ www.
kabul.es ▪ €
Kabul is a favourite with
young backpackers, so it's
often full. Dorm rooms, all
with air conditioning and
some with balconies,
sleep 4–20 people. There's
a gorgeous roof terrace
with hammocks. Other
services include free
Internet access, lockers, a
laundry, and a small café
open during the day.

Mambo Tango

MAP C4 ▪ C/Poeta
Cabanyes 23 ▪ 93 442
51 64 ▪ www.hostel
mambotango.com ▪ €
Former travellers Toto
and Marino are behind
this warm and welcoming
hostel. It has dorms for
four, six, eight and nine
people, breakfast and
sheet-hire are included
in the price, and extras
include complimentary
hot drinks and fruit. Party
animals are actively dis-
couraged, so you can count
on getting a good night's
sleep during your stay.

Primavera Hostel

MAP F2 ▪ C/Mallorca 330
▪ 93 175 21 51 ▪ www.
primavera-hostel.com ▪ €
Full of charming details,
including the original

vaulted ceilings and tiled floors, this hostel offers private and dorm rooms. You can cook in the kitchen and chill out with fellow travellers in the lounge.

Pars Tailor's Hostel

MAP D3 ▪ C/Sepulveda 146 ▪ 93 250 56 84 ▪ https:// parshostels.com ▪ €€
A mother-and-daughter team run this charming hostel, which features vintage interiors designed to evoke a Parisian tailor's in the 1930s. The well-equipped air-conditioned dorms have lockers. There is a terrace, lounge and many free activities.

Beyond Barcelona

Ca l'Aliu

C/Roca 6, Peratallada, 12 km (7.5 miles) NW of Palafrugell ▪ 661 404 935 ▪ www.calaliu.com ▪ €
In the tiny medieval town of Peratallada stands this restored 18th-century *casa rural*. The cosy, comfortable rooms have antique furniture and are all en suite.

Hostal Sa Tuna

Pg de Ancora 6, Platja Sa Tuna, 5 km N of Begur ▪ 97 262 21 98 ▪ Closed Nov–Mar ▪ www.hostal satuna.com ▪ €€
Take in the sea views from your terrace at this stylish, five-room boutique hotel overlooking bays on the Costa Brava. The on-site restaurant serves seafood and other local dishes.

Hotel Aigua Blava

Platja de Fornells, Begur ▪ 97 262 20 58 ▪ Closed mid-Oct–late Mar ▪ www. hotelaiguablava.com ▪ €€
This coastal institution, perched atop rugged cliffs overlooking the

sea, is run by the fourth generation of the same family. Many of the rooms – each individually decorated – have splendid views of the Mediterranean. There's an outdoor pool and breakfast is included in the price. Apartments are also available.

Hotel Aiguaclara

C/Sant Miquel 2, Begur ▪ 97 262 29 05 ▪ www. hotelaiguaclarabegur.com ▪ €€
A historical hotel set in a whitewashed 1866 colonial villa in the centre of town. It was built by a Begur "indiano" – a local nickname for those who made their fortunes in Cuba in the early 19th century. The rooms are a mix of contemporary furnishings and original features. There's a wonderful restaurant and outstanding service.

Hotel Blau Mar

C/Farena 36, Llafranc ▪ 97 261 00 15 ▪ https:// hotelblaumarllafranc. com ▪ €€
Set in a quiet seaside village, Blau Mar has traditionally decorated rooms (most with terraces), lovely gardens and a pool with sea-views. There are several clifftop walks and coves to explore nearby.

Hotel Can Barrina

Ctra de Palautordera al Montseny, km 12, 670, Montseny ▪ 93 847 30 65 ▪ https://canbarrina.com/ en ▪ €€
Built in the 18th century, this farmhouse set in the hills of Montseny, is now an excellent restaurant, which also has a handful of comfortable, rustic rooms. The charming

setting, extensive gardens and an outdoor pool make it the perfect place to relax.

Hotel Històric

C/Belmirall 4a, Girona ▪ 97 222 35 83 ▪ www. hotelhistoric.com ▪ €€
Located in the heart of the old quarter, this is a good base for exploring Girona. Guests have the option of choosing either the rooms or the self-catering apartments.

Parador de Tortosa

Castillo de la Zuda, Tortosa ▪ 97 744 44 50 ▪ www.parador.es ▪ €€
Looming over the town of Tortosa is the ancient Arab Castillo de la Zuda, within which this *parador* is housed. The decor is suitably old-world, with dark-wood furniture and antique fixtures. The view of the countryside and mountains is superb.

Val de Neu

C/Perimetrau s/n ▪ 97 363 50 00 ▪ Closed May– Sep ▪ www.hotelbaqueira valdeneu.com ▪ €€€
A sumptuous ski hotel in the chic resort of Baqueria Beret, Val de Neu is located next to the slopes. Among the five-star amenities are a spa, a pool and an array of restaurants.

Masia Can Pou

Canet d'Adri ▪ 638 18 87 70 ▪ www.masia canpou.com ▪ €€
A traditional Catalan country house, dating back to the 17th-century, this place is now a charming rural retreat. On offer are antique-furnished rooms, a pool and total serenity, despite being just a 20-minute drive from Girona.

For a key to hotel price categories see p142

General Index

Acknowledgments

This edition updated by

Contributor Mary-Ann Gallagher
Senior Editor Alison McGill
Senior Designer Vinita Venugopal
Project Editors Parnika Bagla, Lucy Richards
Project Art Editor Bharti Karakoti
Assistant Editors Tavleen Kaur, Anjasi N.N.
Picture Research Administrator Vagisha Pushp
Picture Research Manager Taiyaba Khatoon
Publishing Assistant Halima Mohammed
Jacket Designer Jordan Lambley
Senior Cartographer Subhashree Bharati
Cartography Manager Suresh Kumar
Senior DTP Designer Tanveer Zaidi
Senior Production Editor Jason Little
Senior Production Controller Samantha Cross
Deputy Managing Editor Beverly Smart
Managing Editors Shikha Kulkarni,
Hollie Teague
Managing Art Editor Sarah Snelling
Senior Managing Art Editor Priyanka Thakur
Art Director Maxine Pedliham
Publishing Director Georgina Dee

DK would like to thank the following for
their contribution to the previous editions:
AnneLise Sorensen, Ryan Chandler, Paula
Canal, Kate Berens, Hilary Bird.

The publisher would like to thank the following
for their kind permission to reproduce their
photographs:
Key: a-above; b-below/bottom; c-centre; f-far;
l-left; r-right; t-top

123RF.com: dudlajzov 59tr; Luciano Mortula 7tr;
Tagstock Japan 14ca.
4Corners: SIME / Pietro Canali 24–5.
Alamy Images: / Alfred Abad 108cl, / Mike
Finn-Kelcey 130tl; Manfred Gottschalk 16–17c;
Hemis 85cl; Hemis / Patrice Hauser 110tl; John
Henshall 27tl; LOOK Die Bildagentur der Fotografen
GmbH / Juergen Richter 43tr; Stefano Politi
Markovina 68bl; Giuseppe Masci 55tr; Hercules
Milas 26-7c; Radharc Images 16br; Sam
Bloomberg-Rissman 69b; Gregory Wrona 78cb.
Alamy Stock Photo: agefotostock / Christian
Goupi 4crb; Greg Balfour Evans 16clb; Peter
Forsberg 90crb; Image Professionals GmbH /
Küppers, Andrea 60tl / Langlotz, Tim 60b, 99tr;
Stefano Politi Markovina 54c, 58tr; Cisco Pelay
79cl; Emily Riddell 81bl; Marc Soler 123br, 121bl;
Topseee 100tr; travelpix 59b; Anton Dos Ventos
104tl; Andrew Wilson 47bl
AWL Images: Sabine Lubenow 2tl, 8–9; Stefano
Politi Markovina 114–5.
Bar Almirall: Bar Almirall 92tl.
Bar del Pla: Bar del Pla 84br.
Bar Muy Buenas: 92br
Bobby Gin: Pau Esculies 122tl.

Boo: 120tl.
Bridgeman Images: Museu d'Art Contemporani de
Barcelona © ADAGP, Paris and DACS, London 2015.
Homea, 1974 Eduardo Arranz Bravo (b.1941) 34br;
Museu Picasso, Barcelona © Succession Picasso/
DACS, London 2015 Harlequin, 1917, Pablo Picasso
(1881–1973) 31tl, Seated Man, 1917, Pablo Picasso
(1881–1973) 31tr; Menu from 'Els Quatre Gats', 1899,
Pablo Picasso (1881–1973) 30bc, Las Meninas,
No.30, 1957, Pablo Picasso (1881–1973) 30–31c.
Bus Terraza: 61br.
Corbis: Ken Welsh 39tr; Gavin Jackson 35cb;
Heritage Images 15tl; JAI / Stefano Politi Markovina
73cla; Jean-Pierre Lescourret 34bl; René Mattes
41tr; Charlie Pérez 54tl; Sylvain Sonnet 18–19c;
Wally McNamee 39bl.
Dorling Kindersley: Museu d'Art Contemporani,
Barcelona © Foundation Antoni Tapies, Barcelone/
VEGAP, Madrid and DACS, London 2015
Deconstructed bed (1992–3) 35tl; Courtesy
of the Palau de la Musica Catalana 33tl.
Dreamstime.com: Igor Abramovych 98cr;
Alexvaneekelen 80tl; Steve Allen 45br, 87br, 95tr;
Danilo Ascione 48tr; Christian Bertrand 55cl, 73tr;
Daniel Sanchez Blasco 87tl; Byelikova 124tl; Catalby
3tr, Charles03 50tl; Juan Bautista Cofreces 64bl;
Demerzel21 96tl; Dennis Dolkens 119bl; Dimbar76 4b;
Dinozzaver 44b; Edufoto 6cla; Ego450 23tl; Elxeneize
116tr; Emotionart 10cla; Alexandre Fagundes De
Fagundes 41clb; Fazon1 10bl, Fotoember 26cb;
Gelia 125tr, Iakov Filimonov 43clb, 52clb, 72br, 72tl;
Christian Horz 68cra; Jackf 50cb, 51b, 70br, 107tr,
126tr, 126–7b; Javarman 4cr, 32cl; Jiawangkun 106tl;
Karsol 12cr, 17cr; Pavel Kavalenkau 71tr; Kemaltaner
4t; Kyolshin 14bl; Lanaufoto 129c; Lavendertime
18cl; Lisja 11tl, Loflo69 128br; Mark52 32–3c, Carlos
Soler Martinez 46bl, Alberto Masnovo 42t; Masterlu
15b; Matteocozzi 40ca; Anamaria Mejia 2tr, 36–7;
Lucian Milasan 96b; Miluxian 22br; Miskolin 118t;
Mkoudis 11crb; Luciano Mortula 45tl; Juan Moyano
40bl, 46t, 48b, 102–3b; Nito100 70tl, 108tr; Andrey
Omelyanchuk 56–7, 88bl; Irina Paley 67tl; Patl
xs4all.nl 22cla; Pathastings 63tr; Photoaliona 28-9c;
Marek Poplawski 71cl, 102tl; Rquemades 4cl;
Sanguer 49tr; Santirf 108–9b; Victor Zastol`skiy 97cl;
Elena Solodovnikova 117tr; Ron Sumners 65tr;
Tanaonte 66b; Thecriss 26br; Tomas1111 7crb;
Toniflap 48c, 76tl; Typhoonski 77tr; Vichie81 12bl;
Vitalyedush 4clb, 95b; Dmitry Volkov 89bl; Yuri4u80
22–3c; Yuryz 27bl.
El Celler de Can Roca: Joan Pujol-Creus 131cb.
Escriba: Escriba 82ca.
Galeria Cosmo: Galeria Cosmo 112t.
Getty Images: Culture Club 38c; Popperfoto 39cla;
Sylvain Sonnet 10tr.
Granja Dulcinea: Granja Dulcinea 65clb.
Holala Ibiza: 91tl
Imanol Ossa: 90c.
iStockphoto.com: MasterLu 5tr, 132–133;
kanuman 3tl, 74–5; thehague 4cla.
Fundacio Joan Miro: © Successió Miró /
ADAGP, Paris and DACS London 2015 11cra,
Catalan Peasant by Moonlight 28bc, Tapis de la
Fundacio 28cl, Sculpture on the Terrace Garden
at Fundacio Joan Miro in Barcelona 29tl.

L'Arca: 82br.
La Manual Alpargatera: 81tc.
La Mar Salada: 105br.
Bar Lobo: Olga Planas 64tr.
Moments/Mandarin Oriental Hotel Group: George Apostolidis 113br.
Dry Martini: Javier de las Muelas 111br.
Metro: 60c.
Milk Bar & Bistro: Duda Bussolin 83cl.
Museu d'Art Contemporani de Barcelona (MACBA): Rafael Vargas 11bl, 34–35c.
Nordik Think: 110cr.
Polaroids: Meg Diaz 83tr.
Photo Scala, Florence: © Succession Picasso / DACS, London 2015 Painting of Margot, or Waiting, 1901 Pablo Picasso 11c.
Shutterstock.com: Jana Asenbrennerova 93, Pajor Pawel 1
SuperStock: DeAgostini Painting of Our Lady of Councilors 1445, by Lluis Dalmau 10br; Fine Art Images The Virgin of Humility (Madonna dell' Umilita) Angelico, Fra Giovanni, da Fiesole (ca. 1400–1455) 20bl; Hemis.fr 33br; Iberfoto /National Art Museum of Catalonia / Painting of The Minuet. 1756. Bequest of Francesc Camb by TIEPOLO, Giovanni Domenico (1727–1804) 20cr, /Ramon Casas and Pere Romeu on a Tandem. 1897. by CASAS i CARBO, Ramn (1866–1932) 21tl, / Ducat with the image of Philip V (1703). Coin 21cra; JTB Photo 32br; Joan Miro Foundation, Barcelona © Successió Miró / ADAGP, Paris and DACS London 2015. Sculpture gallery display 29cr; Picasso Museum, Barcelona © Succession Picasso / DACS, London 2015 Dwarf Dancer (Nana) (Danseuse Naine (La Nana)) 1901 Pablo Picasso (1881–1973 /Spanish) 30cl.
La Taverna del Clinic: 62t.
Windsor: 62br.

Cover
Front and spine: **Shutterstock.com**: Pajor Pawel.Back: **Shutterstock.com**: Pajor Pawel b; **Dreamstime.com:** Boule13 tr; Iakov Filimonov crb, Javarman tl, Vitalyedush cla.

Pull out map cover
Shutterstock.com: Pajor Pawel.

All other images are: © Dorling Kindersley. For further information see www.dkimages.com.

Commissioned Photography: Max Alexander, Departure Lounge/Ella Milroy, Departure Lounge/ Paul Young, Joan Farre, Heidi Grassley, Alex Robinson, Rough Guides/Ian Aitken, Rough Guides/ Chris Christoforou, Rough Guides/Tim Kavenagh.

Illustrators: Chris Orr & Associates, Lee Redmond.

Penguin
Random
House

First edition 2002

Published in Great Britain by
Dorling Kindersley Limited
DK, One Embassy Gardens, 8 Viaduct
Gardens, London SW11 7BW, UK

The authorised representative in the EEA is
Dorling Kindersley Verlag GmbH. Arnulfstr.
124, 80636 Munich, Germany

Published in the United States by
DK Publishing, 1745 Broadway, 20th Floor,
New York, NY 10019, USA

Copyright © 2002, 2023 Dorling
Kindersley Limited
A Penguin Random House Company

23 24 25 26 10 9 8 7 6 5 4 3 2 1

The publishers cannot accept responsibility
for any consequences arising from the use
of this book, nor for any material on third
party websites, and cannot guarantee that
any website address in this book will be a
suitable source of travel information.

A CIP catalogue record is available
from the British Library.

A catalogue record for this book is available
from the Library of Congress.

ISSN 1479-344X
ISBN 978-0-2416-1862-2

Printed and bound in Malaysia.

www.dk.com

As a guide to abbreviations in visitor information
blocks: **Adm** = admission charge; **D** = dinner;
L = lunch.

MIX
Paper | Supporting
responsible forestry
FSC **FSC™ C018179**

This book was made with Forest
Stewardship Council™ certified
paper – one small step in DK's
commitment to a sustainable future.
**For more information go to
www.dk.com/our-green-pledge**

English-Catalan Phrase Book

In an Emergency

Help!	Auxili!	ow-gzee-lee
Stop!	Pareu!	pah-reh-oo
Call a doctor!	Telefoneu un metge!	teh-leh-fon-eh-oo oon meh-djuh
Call an ambulance!	Telefoneu una ambulància!	teh-leh-fon-eh-oo oo-nah ahm-boo-lahn-see-ah
Call the police!	Telefoneu la policia	teh-leh-fon-eh-oo lah poh-lee-see-ah
Call the fire brigade!	Telefoneu els bombers!	teh-leh-fon-eh-oo uhlz boom-behs
Where is the nearest telephone?	On és el telèfon més proper?	on-ehs uhl tuh-leh fon mehs proo-peh
Where is the nearest hospital?	On és l'hospital més proper?	on-ehs looss-pee-tahl mehs proo-peh

Communication Essentials

Yes	Si	see
No	No	noh
Please	Si us plau	sees plah-oo
Thank you	Gràcies	grah-see-uhs
Excuse me	Perdoni	puhr-thoh-nee
Hello	Hola	oh-lah
Goodbye	Adéu	ah-they-oo
Good night	Bona nit	bo-nah neet
Morning	El matí	uhl muh-tee
Afternoon	La tarda	lah tahr-thuh
Evening	El vespre	uhl vehs-pruh
Yesterday	Ahir	ah-ee
Today	Avui	uh-voo-ee
Tomorrow	Demà	duh-mah
Here	Aquí	uh-kee
There	Allà	uh-lyah
What?	Què?	keh
When?	Quan?	kwahn
Why?	Per què?	puhr keh
Where?	On?	ohn

Useful Phrases

How are you?	Com està?	kom uhs-tah
Very well, thank you.	Molt bé, gràcies.	mol beh grah-see-uhs
Pleased to meet you.	Molt de gust.	mol duh goost
See you soon.	Fins aviat.	feenz uhv-yat
Where is/are . ?	On és/són?	ohn ehs/sohn
How far is it to ?	Quants metres/ kilòmetres hi ha d'aquí a ...?	kwahnz meh-truhs/kee-loh-muh-truhs yah dah-kee uh
Which way to ...?	Per on es va a ...?	puhr on uhs bah ah
Do you speak English?	Parla anglès?	par-luh an-glehs
I don't understand	No l'entenc.	noh luhn-teng
Could you speak more slowly, please?	Pot parlar més a poc a poc, si us plau?	pot par-lah mehs pok uh pok sees plah-oo
I'm sorry.	Ho sento.	oo sehn-too

Useful Words

big	gran	gran
small	petit	puh-teet
hot	calent	kah-len
cold	fred	fred
good	bo	boh
bad	dolent	doo-len
enough	bastant	bahs-tan
well	bé	beh
open	obert	oo-behr
closed	tancat	tan-kat
left	esquerra	uhs-kehr-ruh
right	dreta	dreh-tuh
straight on	recte	rehk-tuh
near	a prop	uh prop
far	lluny	lyoonyuh
up/over	a dalt	uh dahl
down/under	a baix	uh bah-eeshh
early	aviat	uhv-yat
late	tard	tahrt
entrance	entrada	uhn-trah-thuh
exit	sortida	soor-tee-thuh
toilet	lavabos/ serveis	luh-vah-boos/ sehr-beh-ees
more	més	mess
less	menys	menyees

Shopping

How much does this cost?	Quant costa això?	kwahn kost ehs-shoh
I would like ...	M'agradaria ...	muh-grah-thuh-ree-ah
Do you have?	Tenen?	tehn-un
I'm just looking, thank you	Només estic mirant, gràcies.	noo-mess ehs-teek mee-rahn grah-see-uhs
Do you take credit cards?	Accepten targes de crèdit?	ak-sehp-tuhn tahr-zhuhs duh kreh-deet
What time do you open?	A quina hora obren?	ah keen-uh oh-ruh oh-bruhn
What time do you close?	A quina hora tanquen?	ah keen-uh oh -ruh tan-kuhn
This one.	Aquest	ah-ket
That one.	Aquell	ah-kehl
That's fine.	Està bé.	uhs-tah beh
expensive	car	kahr
cheap	bé de preu/ barat	beh thuh preh-oo/bah-rat
size (clothes)	talla/mida	tah-lyah/ mee-thuh
size (shoes)	número	noo-mehr-oo
white	blanc	blang
black	negre	neh-gruh
red	vermell	vuhr-mel
yellow	groc	grok
green	verd	behrt
blue	blau	blah-oo
antique store	antiquari/ botiga d'antiguitats	an-tee-kwah-ree/ boo-tee-gah/ dan-tee-ghee-tats
bakery	el forn	uhl forn
bank	el banc	uhl bang

book store	la llibreria	lah lyee-bruh-**ree**-ah
butcher's	la carnisseria	lah kahr-nee-suh-**ree**-uh
pastry shop	la pastisseria	lah pahs-tee-suh-**ree**-uh
chemist's	la farmàcia	lah fuhr-**mah**-see-ah
fishmonger's	la peixateria	lah peh-shuh-tuh-**ree**-uh
greengrocer's	la fruiteria	lah froo-ee-tuh-**ree**-uh
grocer's	la botiga de queviures	lah boo-**tee**-guh duh keh-vee-**oo**-ruhs
hairdresser's	la perruqueria	lah peh-roo-kuh-**ree**-uh
market	el mercat	uhl muhr-**kat**
newsagent's	el quiosc de premsa	uhl kee-**ohsk** duh **prem**-suh
post office	l'oficina de correus	loo-fee-**see**-nuh duh koo-**reh**-oos
shoe store	la sabateria	lah sah-bah-tuh-**ree**-uh
supermarket	el supermercat	uhl soo-puhr-muhr-**kat**
travel agency	l'agència de viatges	la-**jen**-see-uh duh vee-**ad**-juhs

Sightseeing

art gallery	la galeria d'art	lah gah-luh-**ree**-yuh **dart**
cathedral	la catedral	lah kuh-tuh-**thrahl**
church	l'església	luhz-**gleh**-zee-uh
garden	el jardí	uhl zhahr-**dee**
library	la biblioteca	lah bee-blee-oo-**teh**-kuh
museum	el museu	uhl moo-**seh**-oo
tourist information office	l'oficina de turisme	loo-fee-**see**-nuh thuh too-**reez**-muh
town hall	l'ajuntament	luh-djoon-tuh-**men**
closed for holiday	tancat per vacances	tan-**kat** puhr bah-**kan**-suhs
bus station	l'estació d'autobusos	luhs-tah-see-**oh** dow-toh-**boo**-zoos
railway station	l'estació de tren	luhs-tah-see-**oh** thuh **tren**

Staying in a Hotel

Do you have a vacant room?	¿Tenen una habitació lliure?	teh-nuhn oo-nuh ah-bee-tuh-see-**oh** lyuh-ruh
double room with double bed	habitació doble amb llit de matrimoni	ah-bee-tuh-see-**oh** doh-bluh am lyeet duh mah-tree-**moh**-nee
twin room	habitació amb dos llits/ amb llits individuals	ah-bee-tuh-see-**oh** am **dohs** lyeets/am lyeets in-thee-vee-thoo-**ahls**
single room	habitació individual	ah-bee-tuh-see-**oh** een-dee-vee-thoo-**ahl**
room with	habitació	ah-bee-tuh-see-**oh**
a bath shower porter key	amb bany dutxa el grum la clau	am **bah**nyuh **doo**-chuh uhl **groom** lah **klah**-oo
I have a reservation	Tinc una habitació reservada	ting oo-nuh ah-bee-tuh-see-**oh** reh-sehr-**vah**-thah

Eating Out

Have you got a table for…	Tenen taula per…?	**teh**-nuhn **tow**-luh puhr
I would like to reserve a table.	Voldria reservar una taula.	vool-**dree**-uh reh-sehr-**vahr** oo-nuh **tow**-luh
The bill please	El compte, si us plau.	uhl **kohm**-tuh sees plah-oo
I am a vegetarian	Sóc vegetarià/ vegetariana	**sok** buh-zhuh-tuh-ree-**ah**/buh-zhuh-tuh-ree-**ah**-nah
waitress	cambrera	kam-**breh**-ruh
waiter	cambrer	kam-**breh**
menu	la carta	lah **kahr**-tuh
fixed-price menu	menú del migdia	muh-**noo** thuhl meech-**dee**-uh
wine list	la carta de vins	ah **kahr**-tuh thuh **veens**
glass of water	un got d'aigua	oon **got** dah-ee-gwah
glass of wine	una copa de vi	oo-nuh **ko**-pah thuh **vee**
bottle	una ampolla	oo-nuh am-**pol**-yuh
knife	un ganivet	oon gun-ee-**veht**
fork	una forquilla	oo-nuh foor-**keel**-yuh
spoon	una cullera	oo-nuh kool-**yeh**-ruh
breakfast	l'esmorzar	les-moor-**sah**
lunch	el dinar	uhl dee-**nah**
dinner	el sopar	uhl soo-**pah**
main course	el primer plat	uhl pree-**meh** **plat**
starters	els entrants	uhlz ehn-**tranz**
dish of the day	el plat del dia	uhl **plat** duhl **dee**-uh
coffee	el cafè	uhl kah-**feh**
rare	poc fet	**pok fet**
medium	al punt	ahl **poon**
well done	molt fet	mol **fet**

Menu Decoder

l'aigua mineral	lah-ee-gwuh mee-nuh-**rahl**	mineral water
sense gas/ amb gas	sen-zuh gas/ am gas	still sparkling
al forn	ahl **forn**	baked
l'all	**lah**lyuh	garlic
l'arròs	lahr-**roz**	rice
les botifarres	lahs **boo**-tee-fah-rahs	sausages

la carn	*lah karn*	meat
la ceba	*lah seh-buh*	onion
la cervesa	*lah-sehr-ve-sah*	beer
l'embotit	*lum-boo-teet*	cold meat
el filet	*uhl fee-let*	sirloin
el formatge	*uhl for-mah-djuh*	cheese
fregit	*freh-zheet*	fried
la fruita	*lah froo-ee-tah*	fruit
els fruits secs	*uhlz froo-eets seks*	nuts
les gambes	*lahs gam-bus*	prawns
el gelat	*uhl djuh-lat*	ice cream
la llagosta	*lah lyah-gos-tah*	lobster
la llet	*lah lyet*	milk
la llimona	*lah lyee-moh-nah*	lemon
la llimonada	*lah lyee-moh-nah-tuh*	lemonade
la mantega	*lah mahn-teh-gah*	butter
el marisc	*uhl muh-reesk*	seafood
la menestra	*lah muh-nehs-truh*	vegetable stew
l'oli	*loll-ee*	oil
les olives	*luhs oo-lee-vuhs*	olives
l'ou	*loh-oo*	egg
el pa	*uhl pah*	bread
el pastís	*uhl pahs-tees*	pie/cake
les patates	*lahs pah-tah-tuhs*	potatoes
el pebre	*uhl peh-bruh*	pepper
el peix	*uhl pehsh*	fish
el pernil salat serrà	*uhl puhr-neel suh-lat sehr-rah*	cured ham
el plàtan	*uhl plah-tun*	banana
el pollastre	*uhl poo-lyah-struh*	chicken
la poma	*la poh-mah*	apple
el porc	*uhl pohr*	pork
les postres	*lahs pohs-truhs*	dessert
rostit	*rohs-teet*	roast
la sal	*lah sahl*	salt
la salsa	*lah sahl-suh*	sauce
les salsitxes	*lahs sahl-see-chuhs*	sausages
sec	*sehk*	dry
la sopa	*lah soh-puh*	soup
el sucre	*uhl-soo-kruh*	sugar
la taronja	*lah tuh-rohn-djuh*	orange
el te	*uhl teh*	tea
les torrades	*lahs too-rah-thuhs*	toast
la vedella	*lah veh-theh-lyuh*	beef
el vi blanc	*uhl bee blang*	white wine
el vi negre	*uhl bee neh-gruh*	red wine
el vi rosat	*uhl bee roo-zaht*	rosé wine
el vinagre	*uhl bee-nah-gruh*	vinegar
el xai/el be	*uhl shahee/ uhl beh*	lamb
la xocolata	*lah shoo-koo-lah-tuh*	chocolate
el xoriç	*uhl shoo-rees*	red sausage

Numbers

0	zero	*seh-roo*
1	un (masc) una (fem)	*oon oon-uh*
2	dos (masc) dues (fem)	*dohs doo-uhs*
3	tres	*trehs*
4	quatre	*kwa-truh*
5	cinc	*seeng*
6	sis	*sees*
7	set	*set*
8	vuit	*voo-eet*
9	nou	*noh-oo*
10	deu	*deh-oo*
11	onze	*on-zuh*
12	dotze	*doh-dzuh*
13	tretze	*treh-dzuh*
14	catorze	*kah-tohr-dzuh*
15	quinze	*keen-zuh*
16	setze	*set-zuh*
17	disset	*dee-set*
18	divuit	*dee-voo-eet*
19	dinou	*dee-noh-oo*
20	vint	*been*
21	vint-i-un	*been-tee-oon*
22	vint-i-dos	*been-tee-dohs*
30	trenta	*tren-tah*
31	trenta-un	*tren-tah oon*
40	quaranta	*kwuh-ran-tuh*
50	cinquanta	*seen-kwahn-tah*
60	seixanta	*seh-ee-shan-tah*
70	setanta	*seh-tan-tah*
80	vuitanta	*voo-ee-tan-tah*
90	noranta	*noh-ran-tah*
100	cent	*sen*
101	cent un	*sent oon*
102	cent dos	*sen dohs*
200	dos-cents dues-centes (fem)	*dohs-sens doo-uhs sen-tuhs*
300	tres-cents	*trehs-senz*
400	quatre-cents	*kwah-truh-senz*
500	cinc-cents	*seeng-senz*
600	sis-cents	*sees-senz*
700	set-cents	*set-senz*
800	vuit-cents	*voo-eet-senz*
900	nou-cents	*noh-oo-cenz*
1,000	mil	*meel*
1,001	mil un	*meel oon*

Time

one minute	un minut	*oon mee-noot*
one hour	una hora	*oo-nuh oh-ruh*
half an hour	mitja hora	*mee-juh oh-ruh*
Monday	dilluns	*dee-lyoonz*
Tuesday	dimarts	*dee-marts*
Wednesday	dimecres	*dee-meh-kruhs*
Thursday	dijous	*dee-zhoh-oos*
Friday	divendres	*dee-ven-druhs*
Saturday	dissabte	*dee-sab-tuh*
Sunday	diumenge	*dee-oo-men-juh*